A VISION OF

HOPE

Catholic Schooling in Massachusetts

PIONEER INSTITUTE
PUBLIC POLICY RESEARCH

Pioneer Institute

Pioneer's *mission* is to develop and communicate dynamic ideas that advance prosperity and a vibrant civic life in Massachusetts and beyond.

Pioneer's *vision of success* is a state and nation where our people can prosper and our society thrive because we enjoy world-class options in education, healthcare, transportation, and economic opportunity, and where our government is limited, accountable, and transparent.

Pioneer *values* an America where our citizenry is well-educated and willing to test our beliefs based on facts and the free exchange of ideas, and committed to liberty, personal responsibility, and free enterprise.

PIONEER INSTITUTE
PUBLIC POLICY RESEARCH

Contents

Foreword:
The Educational Pilgrimage of Pope St. John Paul II and Its Impact on the World

By George Weigel

Pope St. John Paul II revered the life of the mind and had a profound respect for the educators who helped ignite the flame of learning in their students. That reverence was born in part from the challenging circumstances of his educational journey as both student and university teacher.

After displaying exceptional intellectual gifts in elementary and secondary school, Karol Wojtyła had begun what promised to be a brilliant university career when the venerable Jagiellonian University in Cracow was shuttered by the Nazis in 1939. The university quickly reconstituted itself as an underground institution, but many of its distinguished professors would die in concentration camps during World War II.

After the war, Wojtyła took his first doctorate in Rome at the Pontifical University of St. Thomas Aquinas, the "Angelicum," and later completed a second doctorate at the Jagiellonian. Immediately after Wojtyła received his degree, the university's theology department was closed by the communist government of Poland.

From 1954 until his election as pope, Wojtyła taught at the Catholic University of Lublin — in those days the only genuinely free institution of higher learning between Berlin and Vladivostok. These exceptional experiences of education under pressure deepened Karol Wojtyła's love of learning, his respect for the craft of teaching, and his commitment to courage in thinking boldly.

As pope, John Paul II issued two apostolic constitutions on the reform of Catholic higher education — *Sapientia Christiana* (*Christian Wisdom*) and *Ex Corde Ecclesiae* (*From the Heart of the Church*) — and dedicated his 13th encyclical, *Fides et Ratio* (*Faith and Reason*), to a penetrating exploration of the ways in which religious belief and the intellectual life are mutually enriching. Those magisterial documents repay a close reading.

But for the purposes of this important book on Catholic schools in the Commonwealth of Massachusetts, it may be more useful to take a narrative approach and walk with John Paul II through his educational experiences, with an eye toward drawing some lessons from that journey for our own time.

Classical Education in Wadowice: Culture Drives History

Decades of "Polish jokes" have blinded too many people to the fact that Poland has long been home to a rich and sophisticated high culture, which played a crucial role in keeping the idea of "Poland" alive after Russia, Prussia, and Austria completed the vivisection of the Polish state in the Third Polish Partition of 1795. For the next 123 years, the word "Poland" disappeared from the map of Europe. But during that time of political exile, Polish literature, Polish painting, Polish theater, Polish graphic arts, Polish linguistics, and Polish achievements in philosophy and mathematics helped Poland the nation survive the destruction of Poland the state.

Thus, when the Second Polish Republic emerged from the chaos of a broken Europe at the end of World War I, its schools could draw on a well-developed high culture in a variety of fields. Young Karol Wojtyła, born in the first years of the first independent Poland in a century and a quarter, was a beneficiary of that high culture and the educational system it shaped.

He enjoyed an excellent, classical education in Wadowice, the provincial town some 35 miles west of Cracow where he grew up. There, Latin and Greek were assumed to be part of any proper secondary education, as were demanding studies in the other liberal arts; the memorization and public recitation of poetry was another feature of this form of education that would later serve the future pope well.

And at the same time Wojtyła and his classmates in Wadowice's elementary and secondary schools were immersed in the study of Polish history and culture, the Catholic youngsters in the town received a rigorous catechetical education before receiving their first Holy Communion and the sacrament of Confirmation.

Wadowice was 20 percent Jewish, and the town's reputation for interreligious tolerance also left its mark on its young men and women—none more so than the son of Wadowice who would reconfigure the landscape of the Jewish-Catholic dialogue as pope.

In his first 12 years of schooling in Wadowice, a seed of insight was planted in Karol Wojtyła, and from that seed would grow an idea central to his papal social doctrine and his papal action on the world stage: the conviction that culture, not politics or economics, is the most dynamic force in history.

Culture can be regenerating (as it proved to be in making possible Poland's reclamation of its independence in 1918); culture can be destructive (as the decadent culture of Weimar Germany proved to be in midwifing the Third Reich). But one way or another, culture shapes political and economic life, for good or for ill.

Wojtyła would not have put it in these terms when he left Wadowice in 1938 to begin his university studies in Cracow, but his education in Wadowice had already set him on the intellectual path by which he would confound the Jacobin heresy (politics, understood as the quest for power, drives history) and the Marxist heresy (history is driven by the exhaust fumes of economic processes). In his mature thought, he would insist that culture is the driver of history over time — and at the heart of a regenerative culture is its capacity to instill in students a love of learning and a reverence for the truth.

The Jagiellonian University and World War II: Education as Resistance to Tyranny

The first-class classical education that Karol Wojtyła received at the elementary and secondary levels was one expression of the potency of a Polish high culture that had displayed great regenerative force in helping liberate his country. Sadly, that power was soon put to another test a mere two decades after Poland regained its independence.

For after the Nazi and Soviet invasions of September 1939, "Poland" once again disappeared from maps of Europe: the country was partitioned between two totalitarian monstrosities, one part of it absorbed into an expanded Nazi Germany, another part into the Soviet Union, and a third part left as a killing ground in which the Poles were to be worked into oblivion for the greater glory of the Thousand Year Reich, while Jews from all over Europe and others the Nazis deemed *Untermenschen* were slaughtered by the millions in extermination camps.

Before that horror descended upon Poland, Karol Wojtyła was only permitted one normal year of university education, during which he undertook demanding studies in Polish philology. At the same time, he recounts in his memoir *Gift and Mystery*, he was absorbed by a "passion for theater." He had begun acting and writing plays in Wadowice, and in Cracow he pursued both passions, acting in student productions at the Jagiellonian and composing dramas of his own.

After the university was closed by the Nazis, and amidst his work as a manual laborer in a quarry and a chemical factory, Wojtyła was a central figure in the underground "Rhapsodic Theater," a part of the cultural resistance to the Nazi occupation. The Rhapsodists, as they were known, sponsored clandestine performances of the great works of Polish drama and recitations of classical Polish poetry, all to keep the idea of "Poland" alive so that, postwar, a new, independent Poland could be established on a firm cultural foundation. The experience of wartime Poland — "humiliation at the hands of evil," as John Paul once put it to me — and of resistance through drama and literature would have a lasting effect on the young Pole, and ultimately on the Church and the world.

Sir John Gielgud once remarked that Pope John Paul II had the best sense of timing he had ever seen; Sir Alec Guinness remembered John Paul's exceptionally sonorous speaking voice. The skills recognized by those two great actors were certainly honed by Karol Wojtyła's theatrical experience in Cracow, before and during World War II. Yet the clandestine student/actor/ playwright took from his "passion for theater" more than a set of useful skills: he took a view of the world and the moral life.

Wojtyła learned from his experience of the drama that life itself has an inherently "dramatic" structure, for each of us lives every day in the gap between the person I am and the person I ought to be. To shorten that gap is the work of a lifetime, informed by conscience and reinforced by grace. That dramatic process will lead to human flourishing, happiness, and ultimately beatitude if the "actors" we all are cooperate, through both faith and reason, with the truths that are built into the world and into us — by a loving Creator, Christians would say, who also enters the drama of history as Redeemer, to set the human drama back on its proper course.

University Chaplain: Creating Zones of Freedom for Students

After his ordination to the priesthood in 1946 and two years of graduate study in Rome, Karol Wojtyła returned to Cracow, where Cardinal Adam Stefan Sapieha directed him to create a new ministry to university students at the height of Stalinist repression in Poland. This was dangerous work, as organized

Catholic activities with young people were banned by the communist regime. But Father Wojtyła was very good at it, and his experience as a university chaplain left an indelible mark on his understanding that true education forms good habits of the heart as well as useful skills and good habits of the mind.

He organized clandestine seminars in which students could read and discuss great classical and Christian texts and thus find an antidote to communist propaganda. He broke centuries of clericalist taboos by going skiing, hiking, camping, and kayaking with his young friends, holiday trips on which he created zones of freedom in which anything and everything could be discussed openly. And in this mutual exchange of intellectual and spiritual gifts, he formed strong young Catholics under exceptionally difficult conditions, even as those young people were forming him into one of the most creative, dynamic young priests in the world.

From this chaplaincy experience, Karol Wojtyła took two convictions that would shape his papal ministry and his thinking about education.

First, he came to understand that young people want to be challenged to heroism. Thus when, as pope, he created World Youth Days around the world, he repeated time and again a challenge to the millions of young adults who flocked to be with him: Never, ever settle for less than the spiritual and moral grandeur that the grace of God makes possible in your life. You will fail; we all do. But that is no reason to lower the bar of expectation. Pick yourself up, dust yourself off, seek reconciliation; but never, ever settle for anything less than the greatness that is waiting to be born from within you.

And secondly, Wojtyła learned from his young friends in Cracow (and later in his work as a university professor at Lublin) that young people want to love with a pure love, a love that makes oneself into a gift for another even as one receives the gift of another. From this conviction would grow Wojtyła's groundbreaking book on human sexuality, *Love and Responsibility*, and his even more creative *Theology of the Body*, both of which have had a considerable impact on the Church, especially in religious education and sacramental preparation.

The Catholic University of Lublin and the Papacy: Rescuing Humanism

By the time Karol Wojtyła was elected pope in 1978, he had spent 14 years teaching moral philosophy at the Catholic University of Lublin. From that work, which included undergraduate and graduate teaching, the supervision of doctoral dissertations, and intense intellectual interactions with his faculty colleagues, Wojtyła came to another seminal conviction: The crisis of modernity is a crisis in the idea of the human person.

Communism reduced the person to an automaton, a mere cog in an irresistible historical process; that was easily refuted, not least by the incompetence and brutality of communist governance. The real danger to the future, Wojtyła seemed to intuit, was utilitarianism, which reduced the human person to a bundle of desires-to-be-satisfied. Whether the desires in question were economic or sexual, that dumbing down of our humanity was not only personally demeaning; it was socially and politically destructive.

So, in the late modern and postmodern worlds, the Catholic Church had to propose, and to display in the lives of its people, a much nobler view of the human person—a revitalized humanism that looks to Christ as the model of the truly human.

That revitalized humanism, in turn, had to be informed by a fresh conception of the moral life. As modern philosophy after Kant and Hume had decayed into thinking about thinking (and later into an even more self-absorbed thinking about thinking about thinking), ethics had come unglued from reality, Wojtyła and his Lublin colleagues believed.

So, philosophy, and the Church, had to help the world rediscover and explain some things, known to classical Greek philosophy and confirmed by biblical revelation, that make an ennobling humanism possible: There are moral truths built into the world and into us; we can know those truths by reason (and,

Christians would add, by revelation); knowing those truths discloses our duties and the path to genuine human flourishing.

During his papacy, John Paul II would insist that the Magna Carta of the moral life, as Christians understand it, is the Beatitudes. Moral rules or laws are guardrails that guide the journey to beatitude. But those laws and rules will only make sense in contemporary culture if they're presented as moral guides built into the human condition and ready to be discovered, not as laws and rules imposed on us by an arbitrary God.

God did not leave us alone to figure out the good life by ourselves; as John Paul II put it at Mt. Sinai in 2000, the moral law was written by God on the human heart before it was written on tablets of stone. Understood in those terms, the moral life becomes the expression of an authentic humanism, and education rightly understood empowers students to discern, and live by, those guides to happiness and beatitude.

Karol Wojtyła's experience as a university educator also left an imprint on his encyclical *Fides et Ratio*. Faith needs reason, he wrote there, in order to purify faith from superstition. For its part, reason needs faith, or else it will decay into a stale positivism that eventually leads to radical skepticism and nihilism, neither of which is good for human solidarity, much less for democracy and self-governance. The task of education, John Paul II would insist, is to lift us out of the slough of skepticism and relativism and into the bright uplands of the truth. Educators best do that, he would add, by being attentive to both the life of the mind and the life of the soul.

Empowerment for Excellence

Viewed through the lens of John Paul II's educational journey, the continuing relevance of his experience and his teaching for twenty-first century Catholic schools should come into focus.

Catholic schools must be schools for empowerment; schools that begin their work from the premise that students of all backgrounds, and especially students from poor families, are people with potential. That potential—spiritual, intellectual, economic, cultural, and civic — will be unleashed when students are formed morally as well as educated intellectually, when students are empowered to become men and woman of character as well as men of women of competence and culture.

Understanding that in the past, Catholic schools have become the best antipoverty program in the history of the Church in the United States.

Building on that understanding in the future, Catholic schools can lead in the reform that American education so manifestly needs.

May the reflections in this book contribute to that Catholic leadership.

George Weigel is Distinguished Senior Fellow and William E. Simon Chair in Catholic Studies at Washington's Ethics and Public Policy Center. A Catholic theologian and one of America's leading public intellectuals, he is the author of the international bestselling two-volume biography of Pope St. John Paul II, *Witness to Hope* and *The End and the Beginning*. Weigel is the author or editor of more than 20 other books, including *Lessons in Hope: My Unexpected Life with St. John Paul II*. His essays, op-ed columns, and reviews appear regularly in major U.S. newspapers. A frequent guest on television and radio, he is also Senior Vatican Analyst for *NBC News*. His weekly column, "The Catholic Difference," is syndicated to 85 newspapers and magazines in seven countries. Weigel is the recipient of 19 honorary doctorates in divinity, philosophy, law, and social science.

Introduction: Catholic K–12 Education and Its Mission in Twenty-First Century America

By Ambassadors Raymond L. Flynn & Mary Ann Glendon

"You can get all A's and still flunk life,"[1] wrote the great twentieth-century Catholic novelist Walker Percy. The authors in this book have done Catholic educators and families a tremendous service by explaining why the centuries-old traditions of Catholic education is such an invaluable resource for K–12 American schooling.

There are similarities between Catholic schools and public schools, but one profound difference. In addition to providing academic knowledge and skills, Catholic schools have a mission to nurture faith and prepare students to live lives illuminated by a Catholic worldview.

It is that religious focus that makes curricular fads like national curriculum standards and social emotional learning (SEL) particularly ill-suited for Catholic schools.

Catholic schools have traditionally offered a classical liberal arts education that includes religious instruction to aid spiritual development—a combination that generations of grateful parents and students have prized.

Through tales of heroism, self-sacrifice, and mercy in great literature such as *Huckleberry Finn, Sherlock Holmes,* and the works of Dante, Charles Dickens, Jane Austen, Edith Wharton, and C.S. Lewis, Catholic schools seek to impart moral lessons and deep truths about the human condition.

The moral, theological, and philosophical elements of Catholic education have never been more needed than they are today, amid a degrading culture marked by popular entertainment, opioid epidemics, street-gang violence, wide achievement gaps, and explosive racial tensions.

The approach of contemporary secular education is contrary to the best academic studies of language acquisition and human formation. It drastically cuts study of classical literature and poetry, and represents what Magdalen College of the Liberal Arts professor and Dante scholar Anthony Esolen calls a strictly utilitarian view of mankind — "man with the soul amputated."

It undermines the historic achievements of Catholic education and pays little attention to "the true, the good, the beautiful." The occasions for grace that can occur when students encounter literature that immerses them in timeless human experiences are replaced by mere training and production of workers for an economic machine.

The "cold reading" method exemplified in today's national standards transforms literacy into a content-empty "skill set." Its math standards stop short of even a full Algebra II course, leaving students unprepared for serious college coursework in science, technology, engineering, or math.

As 132 Catholic scholars wrote in a letter to the U.S. Catholic bishops, such an approach is "a recipe for standardized workforce preparation"[2] that dramatically diminishes children's intellectual and spiritual horizons.

Catholic education, by contrast, seeks to maximize the intellectual and spiritual potential of every child. Following Pope St. John Paul II, who wrote, "[t]o contemplate Christ involves being able to recognize him wherever he manifests himself,"[3] Catholic education looks for the face of Christ in every person.

Catholic schools believe that all students are better off for reading Dante, Shakespeare, and Flannery O'Connor — whether they plan to become philosophers or welders. All students ought to have the opportunity to study mathematics that can guide a sustained, scientific investigation of creation.

Religion and moral culture are pivotal for our American democratic experiment, upholding the rule of law, creating compassion for the disadvantaged, and fostering social cohesion. Even professed atheist Jürgen Habermas recognized that Western culture cannot abandon its religious heritage without endangering the great social and political advances grounded in that heritage.

Today, it is more urgent than ever to find ways to provide children with the fundamental intellectual, spiritual, and moral ideals necessary for humans to flourish. Indeed, no free society can survive for long without cultivating character and competence in its citizens and public servants.

The introduction of national curriculum standards, SEL, and other elements that mark a shift away from the moral and cultural patrimony of Western Civilization comes at a difficult time for Catholic education.

Since 1990, 300,000 students have been displaced from Catholic schools across the nation, and another 300,000 could lose their schools over the next 20 years.[4] In 1965, 5.2 million students attended Catholic schools. Today that number is closer to two million.[5] Even in heavily Catholic Boston, Catholic schools have declined from 225 in 1942 to just 124 as of 2011 and 100 as of 2020.[6]

These declines cannot be attributed to academics. Boston's Catholic schools beat national test averages and dramatically outperform the Boston Public Schools (BPS). While BPS's graduation rate is less than 80 percent, Archdiocese of Boston schools have a 96 percent college-matriculation rate.

Moreover, Catholic schools provide a refuge for many children who lead otherwise chaotic lives. These schools provide moral and religious education and discipline, characteristics that attract parents of all faiths — nearly 20 percent of students in Archdiocese of Boston schools aren't Catholic.

Many of Catholic education's problems are outside their control. In 1960, three-quarters of Catholic school staff were priests or nuns who worked for little or no pay. Today, only 4 percent of staff are priests or nuns,[7] and Catholic schools must rely on paid lay staff. And many families who once sent their children to Catholic schools have moved to the suburbs and patronize public schools there.

Despite these realities, Catholic schools still provide quality education to thousands who cannot afford private schools or a house in the suburbs. They accommodate as many as possible, even those who cannot pay all — or any — tuition.

As they face numerous challenges, Catholic schools must resist the public school "solutions" that would cause them to lose the distinctiveness that attracts families to them in the first place. Catholic schools should continue to adhere to the best of Catholicism's timeless principles so as to maximize the intellectual and spiritual potential of every student. Each child deserves to be prepared for a God-given life of the imagination and the spirit, one that provides a deep appreciation for knowledge, goodness, beauty, truth, and faith.

The classical Catholic understanding of human flourishing is too precious — and great literature, drama, and poetry too intertwined in the academic and moral underpinnings of a Catholic education — to be sacrificed. It is to be hoped that the present study will help American Catholics to better understand what's really at stake.

Raymond Flynn was a three-term Mayor of Boston and U.S. Ambassador to the Holy See during the Clinton Administration. He also served as a Massachusetts State Representative, on the Boston City Council, and in the U.S. Army. Ambassador Flynn is a leading lay Catholic voice in the United States, a best-selling author of *The Accidental Pope* and *John Paul II: A Personal Portrait of the Pope and the Man*, as well as a frequent newspaper columnist, national TV analyst, and national talk show host. Flynn graduated from Providence College as a Dean's List All-American-Academic. He earned a Master's degree from the Harvard University Graduate School of Education.

Mary Ann Glendon is the Learned Hand Professor of Law, *emerita*, at Harvard University, a former U.S. Ambassador to the Holy See, and a member of the American Academy of Arts and Sciences. Ambassador Glendon chaired the U.S. State Department Commission on Unalienable Rights and served on the U.S. Commission on International Religious Freedom and the U.S. President's Council on Bioethics. She received the National Humanities Medal in 2006. She was President of the Pontifical Academy of Social Sciences (2003–2013), a member of the Board of Supervisors of the Institute of Religious Works (2013–2018), and represented the Holy See at various conferences. Glendon's works include *The Forum and the Tower* (2011), biographical essays exploring the relation between political philosophy and politics-in-action; *Traditions in Turmoil* (2006), a collection of essays on law, culture and human rights; and *A World Made New: Eleanor Roosevelt and the Universal Declaration of Human Rights* (2001).

Chapter 1: "Be Not Afraid": A History of Catholic Education in Massachusetts

By Cara Stillings Candal, Ed.D.

Executive Summary

Catholic schools in Massachusetts have long been important to families of diverse backgrounds and faiths, as evidenced by the numbers of non-Catholics who seek the high-quality academic and values-based education they provide. As Dr. Mary Grassa O'Neill, former secretary of education and superintendent of the Archdiocese of Boston notes, "Catholic education is a vital and important part of society ... Catholic schools achieve excellence in education and Catholic identity, and our schools form good, caring people every day."[8]

In the fall of 2020, there are 183 Catholic schools in Massachusetts, 100 in the Archdiocese of Boston.[9] Their success is manifest in high test scores and high graduation and college attendance rates. Archdiocese elementary Catholic schools educate students at an average per-pupil tuition of $6,583[10] versus the nearly $16,500 per-pupil average for Massachusetts public schools.[11] Catholic school tuitions are often *lower* than the average per-pupil cost to the schools because many serve working- and middle-class families who cannot afford to pay more. Catholic schools also provide generous financial aid to families who cannot afford the average cost of tuition.[12]

Despite their success, Catholic schools are in crisis: In the past five years, 20 schools in the Archdiocese of Boston have closed. The coronavirus (COVID-19) pandemic, despite providing an initial enrollment boost for schools that survived the spring of 2020 and chose to provide live instruction in the fall, could have long-term detrimental consequences for Catholic schools everywhere.[13]

In this chapter we:

- Explore the history of Catholic education in Massachusetts and the Archdiocese, how the Church's educational mission has changed, and factors contributing to financial and enrollment crises.

- Show why Catholic schools should be considered essential partners in education by illustrating their success vis-à-vis public schools.

- Outline efforts by the Catholic community and the Archdiocese to reverse the discouraging trend of Catholic school closures.

- Provide recommendations for the perpetuation of Catholic schools in Massachusetts.

Catholic Schooling in Massachusetts and Boston: A Brief History

The history of Catholic education in Massachusetts traces the city's immigrant, political, and broader public education histories. Catholic schools here embody the educational values of a state that was the first to recognize education as a public good.

In 1825, only one Catholic school existed within what is today the Archdiocese of Boston. Despite an influx of Catholics after 1846, the growth of Catholic schools was slow, in part because of a public-school system viewed by Horace Mann as "an engine of social reform" to help acculturate immigrants.[14] In greater part, however, slow growth was due to anti-Catholic sentiment.[15]

From less than 10 percent Catholic in 1825, Boston was 40 percent Irish by 1850 as immigrants fled famine.[16] These largely poor, Catholic immigrants were seen as problematic by the ruling Protestant elite.

Anti-Catholic sentiment peaked in the 1850s with the formation of political and social groups aimed at preserving Protestant supremacy.[17] The "Know-Nothing" Party supported the 1855 Anti-Aid Amendment[18] that prohibited state monies from flowing to sectarian schools. A 1917 nativist amendment prohibited aid to any institution "not publicly owned and under the exclusive control, order and superintendence" of the state or federal government.[19]

Despite these amendments, between 1900 and the 1940s, Catholic parish schools grew steadily.[20] By 1940, it was clear the parish system needed outside support to meet demand in Boston, then the third largest diocese in the nation, with 158 parish grammar schools and 67 high schools in 1942.[21]

In the 1960s, Archbishop Richard Cushing encouraged "the development of multi-parish diocesan high schools"[22] to lower costs, meet the needs of working-class and poor families, and allow parish priests to continue teaching. *New York Times* columnist John H. Fenton wrote Boston was one of the most well-equipped Catholic parochial school systems in the country.[23]

The 1960s also saw the beginning of a crisis in Catholic education as, with the decline in vocations and the number of priests and nuns available to teach in Catholic schools, the schools increasingly turned to laity who require living wages.[24]

In the 1970s, desegregation of Boston's schools outraged inner-city residents, including many Catholics who questioned the leadership of Archbishop Cardinal Medeiros.[25] Moreover, many Irish and Italian immigrants had moved to the suburbs, where quality public schools lowered demand for Catholic schools.[26]

Between 1965 and 1973, total enrollment in Archdiocese schools fell from 151,562 to 84,769, and many Catholic schools closed.[27] Still, Catholic schools continued to fulfill their mission, serving increasing numbers of African American families[28] and Asian and Caribbean immigrants into the 1980s.[29]

Sociologist James Coleman described how Catholic schooling's culture of high academic expectations served poor and minority students well.[30] Coleman, and later Bryk, Lee, and Holland, in *Catholic Schools and the Common Good*, illustrated how inner-city Catholic schools served all, regardless of ability to pay.[31] Both studies suggested how public schools could learn from Catholic schools how to close achievement gaps between white, middle-class pupils and poor and minority ones.[32]

Some public schools, including charter public schools,[33] emphasize high expectations and accept no excuses for failure.[34] This model, as Bryk, Lee, and Holland note, derives from the Catholic school idea that students can achieve the same academic results regardless of background.[35]

Despite their successes, many Catholic schools are struggling to attract students and funding. In 2010, the Fordham Institute captured the national picture of the Catholic school struggle, finding that since 1990, 300,000 students nationally, most of them residents of inner cities, saw their Catholic schools close for lack of funding.[36] Since that report, another 1,191 schools have closed or consolidated nationwide. While 244 new schools opened prior to 2020,[37] closures after the onset of the COVID-19 pandemic have nearly eradicated that gain, with Catholic elementary schools most impacted.[38]

Massachusetts's Catholic school crisis mirrors the national experience. In Boston alone, 20 Catholic schools have closed since 2015.[39] Since the spring of 2020, 10 Catholic schools have closed across the Commonwealth — victims of enrollment declines exacerbated by the COVID-19 pandemic, when parents who lost jobs were unable to make final tuition payments. Closures are occurring in poor, working-class, and immigrant communities such as Chelsea, Boston, and Lowell.[40] These are places where families feel the loss of their local Catholic school acutely, because the district schools have long struggled to provide families with high-quality educational options.[41]

In the past decade, the Archdiocese of Boston has made several attempts to stem school closures. Leaders say that schools have remained focused on providing an excellent education to the "kids who need it most,"[42] and have revitalized and reinvigorated Catholic education.[43] Efforts have included aligning curricula with Massachusetts's nationally renowned standards and making better use of norm-referenced tests to track achievement.[44]

The Archdiocese has also placed a renewed emphasis on the importance of faith, as exemplified by the Cristo Rey model of high-quality academics with very low tuitions.

While new models are necessary, existing ones also need to be sustained. Catholic schools in Boston enjoy a generous donor community, but relying on philanthropy isn't a sustainable model. Absent a revision to the Anti-Aid Amendment, Catholic school students can only hope politicians understand the import of what Catholic schools offer to communities, both academically and culturally.

The Opportunities and Outcomes of Catholic Education in Massachusetts

Despite considerable challenges and a relatively unchanged[45] education policy environment in Massachusetts, Catholic schools have persisted in providing all students with access to high-quality education thanks to an unrelenting focus on achievement.[46]

The academic success of Catholic schools is manifest in high test scores, high graduation and college attendance rates, low per-pupil costs, and taxpayer savings. In urban centers, Catholic schools provide for populations that are disproportionately poor, minority, lack early childhood education programs, and lack family structures that promote success in school.[47]

Across the Commonwealth, over half of archdiocesan elementary schools are in urban settings. According to Boston Public Schools, of the 29 percent of students living in Boston who choose not to attend the city's public schools, 64 percent are black or Hispanic and roughly 30 percent are enrolled in private and parochial schools inside and outside of Boston (the majority of the rest attend charter public schools).[48]

Catholic schools in Massachusetts do not participate in the

Massachusetts Comprehensive Assessment System (MCAS), but results from norm-referenced[49] assessments that Catholic schools use, along with SAT results, are useful (See Figures 1 and 2). And the Archdiocese has a 96 percent college enrollment rate,[50] compared to 79 percent in the Boston Public Schools.[51]

Academics are not the only basis on which families and students choose schools. Even those families who do not identify as Catholic (18 percent of enrollment) are attracted by the moral and character education. As Principal Monica Haldiman of Sacred Heart Elementary School in Roslindale says, "we are expected to provide a value-laden education," and parents appreciate that we can easily say to students "this is right, and this is wrong."

Figure 1. Stanford 10 Scores, Archdiocese of Boston/Nation (Average All Subjects)[52]

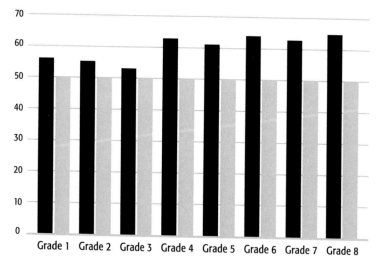

Figure 2. SAT Scores, 2010, Archdiocese of Boston, Boston Public, Massachusetts (Public), the Nation[53]

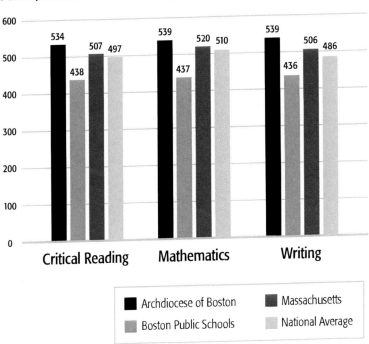

Boston's Catholic elementary schools achieve their mission at an average tuition of just $6,583 per student.[54] But this cost to families doesn't reflect the real per-pupil cost of education, which can be up to $2,000 higher per student. The gap reflects the Archdiocese's commitment to educate students regardless of socioeconomic status, but also poses a financial challenge met in part with the help of private donors and philanthropic organizations.

In the past decade, average per-pupil expenditures in Catholic schools have compared favorably to the state as a whole ($16,500 per pupil) and districts such as Boston, Lawrence, and Quincy, all of which report 2020 expenditures of roughly $14,000 to $21,000 per student. Even after factoring out special education costs, general education in Boston Public Schools is more than $20,000 per pupil—much higher than in Catholic schools.[55]

Such comparisons are useful for understanding the taxpayer savings attributable to the tens of thousands of Massachusetts families choosing Catholic schools. When students enroll in Catholic schools, their families still pay taxes that benefit districts. When districts keep those tax dollars but don't have to educate students, they save hundreds of millions of dollars each year.[56]

Despite the high-quality, low-cost model, Catholic education is impacted by migration to suburbs, decreases in the number of priests and nuns, internal Church politics, and Massachusetts's bar on public assistance to sectarian schools. These and other factors have created a crisis in Catholic education. Father William Leahy, the current president of Boston College, contends Catholic schools in Massachusetts are "one step beyond crisis."[57]

The State of Things: Catholic Schools in Massachusetts

The crisis is most evident in declining enrollments and closed schools, mostly in the state's urban centers, where tuitions range from just 50 percent to about 85 percent of actual per-pupil costs.[58]

Enrollment trends in Catholic schools are part of an overall decline in enrollment in the state as a whole. Since the turn of the century, Massachusetts public schools have lost roughly 30,000 students, with enrollment hovering around 950,000 since 2015. The enrollment decline is more severe in lower-income areas than in middle- or upper-income areas."[59]

While schools across the state are losing enrollment, the numbers of Catholic elementary schools—the bulk of Catholic schools in the Archdiocese—reflect a national downward trend. According to the National Catholic Education Association (NCEA), nationwide enrollment has fallen from 5.2 million in 1965 to about 1.7 million in 2020. Enrollment declines have led to the closure of thousands of schools, including 1,191 schools in the last 10 years alone, many of which were located in the nation's 12 major urban centers for Catholic education, including Boston.[60, 61]

How has this happened? For starters, an increase in numbers of white Catholics moving to the suburbs has left one-third of the overall Catholic population living in urban areas where two-thirds of Archdiocese schools are located—this helps explain why so many urban Catholic schools are under-enrolled or closed.[62] Moreover, many Catholics who left the city feel well served by suburban public schools.

Compounding the financial challenge is the decline in religious vocations. Prior to the 1960s, priests and nuns ran highly effective parish schools while drawing small stipends or no salaries. Over the past 40 years, the teaching burden has shifted dramatically to lay instructors: Religious accounted for 92 percent of Catholic school staff in 1920, 74 percent by 1960, and under 4 percent nationwide in 2010.[63] While many lay staff are outstanding educators and leaders, they do require a salary, even if it is often substantially less than in a public school.

Catholic schools in urban centers with great demand for educational alternatives thus confront the costs of paying faculty and staff while helping families who cannot pay full (or any) tuition. Catholic schools in Boston thus rely heavily on philanthropy, including the Catholic Schools Foundation, the Lynch Foundation, the Campaign for Catholic Schools, and private philanthropists. Many fear that overreliance on philanthropy could result in donor fatigue.[64]

President of Boston College Fr. Leahy admits the crisis reflects the Church's failure both to understand internal changes and plan to invest in education. With regard to high-quality lay teachers and leaders, he notes, "we didn't understand that quality costs."

The growth of charter public schools suggests the extent to which quality counts for parents. Boston-area charter public schools are concentrated in urban centers, attract the same students served by Catholic schools, and have records of success that make them an attractive, free option to families.[65]

Yet charter public schools are not exclusively responsible for enrollment problems in Catholic education. As Katie Everett, executive director of the Lynch Foundation, points out, charter public schools account for only 15 percent of Catholic school attrition. Economist Ken Ardon estimates that, at most, only one-fifth of the decline in public school enrollments can be explained by increasing charter public school enrollments.[66]

However, since charter schools are an attractive alternative for black and Hispanic students,[67] Catholic schools should:

- Differentiate themselves from charters by reemphasizing the benefits of a Catholic education beyond academic excellence
- Look for opportunities to collaborate with charter public school counterparts to reach students.

One way to collaborate, suggest Fr. Leahy and Everett of the Lynch Foundation, is to lease vacant Catholic school buildings to charters, which receive state grants that cover only about 12 percent of building and renovation costs[68] — and reserve after-hours use of the buildings for activities related to Catholic education.[69]

In addition to building relationships with the wider education community, the Archdiocese has implemented financial, quality, and accountability initiatives, including:[70]

- Implementation of common standards based on the (former) Massachusetts Curriculum Frameworks
- Standard use of Stanford 10 tests to track achievement
- More frequent and consistent use of assessment data to drive instruction
- Creation of an Elementary Schools Task Force to provide "a private, comprehensive analysis of the financial status of all elementary schools in the Archdiocese" and give each school "new financial management tools to serve as a road map to long-term financial stability."[71]

These initiatives are especially important in Boston, where the public schools are beginning to benefit from years of intense local reform and state policy initiatives. The Archdiocese is keen to ensure that schools and teachers view new academic standards as the "floor, not the ceiling."[72]

Additional initiatives have focused on teacher support and professional development, improving school facilities and access to technology, and expanding academic programming. One professional development effort comes out of Boston College, home to the Urban Catholic Teachers' Corps, a program that recruits young teachers to spend two years in an inner-city Catholic school.[73]

The Archdiocese is merging small, struggling schools into regional academies that are governed by regional boards charged with making autonomous decisions about budgets, enrollment, and academics. Academies have been created in Dorchester, Brockton, Lawrence, Quincy, and South Boston, helping ensure Catholic schools remain open to those who need them most.[74]

For families who rely upon Catholic schools as a high-quality educational option, a broader political problem exists: Aside from modest federal support for early childhood education, they receive no government support. They must therefore pay both the cost of Catholic school and taxes to support the local public school. Moreover, Catholic schools continue to bear financial burdens as they commit to "serving the children most in need." As one Catholic school leader notes, "that is the mission-driven aspect of our work."[75]

Resolving the Crisis: Recommendations for the Perpetuation of Catholic Schools

Massachusetts policy makers have much to learn from Catholic schools, but adopting a Catholic school model in secular public schools will not confer the non-academic benefits that Catholic schools offer. Policy makers continue to ignore both the right of families to choose the schools they prefer and the excellence Catholic schools provide.

If Catholic schools are to survive, change must come from within. The Archdiocese has made admirable strides in creating educational models that are more financially viable, but must consider additional ways to increase quality, control costs, and continue to serve families who seek Catholic schooling. The following recommendations are for policy makers and the Catholic schools community in Massachusetts.

Repeal Massachusetts's Two Anti-Aid Amendments

The 1855 and 1917 Anti-Aid Amendments to the Massachusetts Constitution are relics of a shameful time and should be repealed. While, as the Fordham Institute points out, "vouchers should not be viewed as a panacea,"[76] prohibiting families from exercising their rights hurts families, students, and taxpayers, who are forced to support an expensive public system that doesn't work for all students. It is not tenable for Catholic schools to continue providing a high-quality education to all without state support. Given that Massachusetts taxpayers save hundreds of millions due to children attending Catholic schools, they have an interest in seeing these schools survive and thrive.[77]

Enact Tuition Tax Credits for Families Using Religious and Independent Schools

Implementing tuition tax credits for families who choose private education is a just way to compensate families who opt out of the public system but pay taxes. Both Rhode Island and Florida give substantial tax breaks to corporations that support not-for-profit scholarship organizations that provide scholarships to private schools or transportation scholarships to out-of-district public schools.

Continue to Reach Out to the Catholic Community and Beyond

Beyond reengaging Catholics outside of the inner city, Catholic schools need to form relationships with non-Catholic and public schools. Charter public schools are both a model and potential partner, as they receive full per-pupil operational funding, but only small grants toward capital costs. Many charters reach out to corporations, private donors, and their communities. There is a sense in the Catholic community that if Catholic schools were to market themselves better, they could draw greater financial support and pressure policy makers for change.

In addition, the Archdiocese has many vacant buildings they could lease to charter public schools to raise funds for diocesan schools. Where there is not enough demand for a Catholic school per se, buildings could be leased during the day, and space reserved for Catholic educational purposes after school hours.

Expand Relationships with University Partners

The Archdiocese could expand already the strong relationships it has with many area colleges[78] to assist in the creation and implementation of teacher and school leader programs, to gather and interpret data to assist in decision-making, and to reach out to students across the university who are future Catholic school teachers and leaders.

Continue to Emphasize the Importance of a High-Quality Education for All Students

Catholic schools should continue to pursue their mission to educate all children to the highest possible standard, regardless of family background or ability to pay. A continued emphasis on standards, accountability, and professional development coupled with a willingness to "sell" these aspects of Catholic education to the public will result in increased enrollments.

In this vein, the creation of a school system in which schools can be more easily tracked and compared to one another via a common set of standards and testing will establish a strong system of accountability, guiding decisions regarding school performance and closures.

Concentrate on the Provision of Distinctive Catholic School Options

As the public system in Boston earns a better reputation and as high-quality charter school options are expanded, Catholic schools in Boston and beyond should continue to offer the one thing public schools cannot—a Catholic education. Moreover, the Catholic community should continue to support innovation in Catholic schooling by fostering growth of the Cristo Rey and Nativity Miguel networks. By continuing to positively differentiate themselves from the public system, such Catholic schools will remain attractive to certain communities and students.

✖ ✖ ✖

Cara Stillings Candal, Ed.D., has spent the last 10 years working in education policy as a Senior Fellow with both Pioneer Institute and the Center for Education Reform. She was also a founding team member of the National Academy of Advanced Teacher Education (NAATE) and a research assistant professor at Boston University in the Department of Educational Leadership and Development. Candal has authored/edited more than 25 papers and three books on education policy. She earned a Bachelor of Arts in English Literature from Indiana University, a Master of Arts in Social Science from the University of Chicago, and a Doctor of Education from Boston University. Candal is the author most recently of Pioneer Institute's book, *The Fight for the Best Charter Public Schools in the Nation*.

Chapter 2:
The Know-Nothing Amendments: Barriers to School Choice in Massachusetts

By Cornelius (Con) Chapman

"I am not a Know-nothing. How could I be? When the Know-nothings get control, the Declaration of Independence will read 'all men are created equal, except negroes and foreigners and Catholics.' "
— Abraham Lincoln, letter to Joshua Speed, 1855

Author's note: This chapter is based on a paper written in 2009, more than a decade before the Supreme Court's 2020 decision in *Espinoza v. Montana Department of Revenue.* While it anticipated the result in that case and the basis for the court's holding in the Free Exercise Clause of the First Amendment to the U.S. Constitution, it offered other theories for challenging state constitutional Blaine Amendments. The utility of these additional lines of argument has been diminished by *Espinoza*, in which the court recognized the Free Exercise Clause as a sufficient basis for challenging a state prohibition against aid to schools on religious grounds. This chapter has been revised to reflect *Espinoza* without abandoning its original suggested alternatives to the Free Exercise Clause, as they may be useful in situations where a child is injured by a state limitation on educational aid, but a religious standard is absent (e.g., a school funding formula that treats charter schools less favorably than non-charter schools).

Introduction

Consider a sad phenomenon in American history—nineteenth-century nativism and anti-Catholic prejudice—and its lingering and deleterious effects on American education. The wave of nativist sentiment that swept through American thought and institutions in the nineteenth century wiped out an older, pluralistic approach to primary and secondary education in which the interests of parents were balanced with those of the state.

The purported constitutional grounds for this shift rest on an incorrect assumption as to whether the framers of the Constitution intended to include education within the prohibition of established religions. As a correction, this chapter will examine more pragmatic standards for the evaluation of church-state controversies in K–12 education which place the Free Exercise Clause of the First Amendment on an equal footing with that amendment's Establishment Clause.

American Schools: A Brief History

America's public schools were originally religious in nature. In a published debate in leading educational journals between 1891 and 1893, the point of contention was not whether primary and secondary education in America had religious roots, but who should receive the credit—the Puritans of Massachusetts or the Protestant Dutch of New York.[79]

The American colonies were imbued with religious coloration from their birth. The charters granted to the colonies by the English Crown had authorized established, state-supported religions. As the United States Supreme Court noted in *Reynolds v. United States*:

"Before the adoption of the [U.S.] Constitution... The people were taxed, against their will, for the support of religion, and sometimes for the support of particular sects to whose tenets they could not and did not subscribe."[80]

The Massachusetts Constitution of 1780 provided for the "support and maintenance of public Protestant teachers of piety, religion and morality."[81] In Massachusetts, public school was Protestant school.[82]

The framers of the United States Constitution, by contrast, started afresh, and the First Amendment prohibited Congress from making any law respecting "an establishment of religion, or prohibiting the free exercise thereof."

State constitutional provisions that established particular religions were not prohibited until the Fourteenth Amendment was interpreted to require the application of the Bill of Rights to the states.[83]

In 1779, Virginian George Mason resolved the church-state controversy with a bill that permanently suspended ministers' state salaries, but left property purchased with state funds in the hands of the Anglican Church.[84]

If Mason was considered a liberal on church-state, Thomas Jefferson was considered an arch-liberal[85] who showed a "passion for religious liberty."[86] Jefferson's letter to the Danbury Baptist Association crystallized the image of "a wall of separation between church and State."[87] Yet even Jefferson did not draw that line through the schoolhouse.

In 1822, Jefferson recommended religious denominations be permitted "to establish their religious schools" on the grounds of the University of Virginia. Jefferson believed that the support of religious education was a proper function of the state and permissible under the First Amendment so long as no one religion was preferred.[88]

The Nativist Reaction to Nineteenth-Century Immigration

Between 1815 and 1865, approximately five million Europeans immigrated to the United States. Many German, English, Norwegian, and Swedish newcomers had resources to sustain themselves until they could move inland and buy land.

The Irish, however, had been impoverished by measures dating to the seventeenth century. Between 1820 and 1860, one-third of immigrants to America were Irish, driven from their country by poverty and famine. They largely settled in the East Coast ports where they arrived. By 1850, the Irish population of Boston had increased to 50,000.[89] Lacking capital and skills, the Irish became a visible social problem in urbanized Boston and the first targets of a native animus that would solidify a rigid educational uniformity that persists in America today.

The Protestant elite that ruled Massachusetts became alarmed by the influx of Irish Catholic immigrants. Public health concerns over the squalor in which the immigrants lived was heightened by anti-Catholicism, a legacy of religious conflict dating to sixteenth-century England.[90]

Nativist sympathizers formed groups to preserve Protestant supremacy, including the American Party.[91] Because members pledged not to give out information about the party, it was called the "Know-Nothing Party." Members would greet any inquiry by replying "I know nothing."

In 1854, the Know-Nothings gained control of the Massachusetts Legislature and the State House. The Know-Nothings' most enduring accomplishment is an 1855 amendment to the Massachusetts Constitution that provided that state appropriations and local tax revenues "… shall never be appropriated to any religious sect for the maintenance exclusively of its own schools."[92]

Until 1833, the Massachusetts Constitution had permitted an individual to direct levies required to support "public Protestant teachers" to "teachers of his own religious sect or denomination."[93] Thus, in 1829, Catholics had begun to organize their own schools and doubled enrollment within six years.[94]

Protestants feared that Catholic schools would grow to demand a share of public monies as had happened in New York and Philadelphia, touching off anti-Catholic riots.[95] The Declaration of Rights of the Massachusetts Constitution was amended in 1833 to remove the provisions relating to education, and the Anti-Aid Amendment placed school funding beyond the reach of the Legislature.[96]

Yet schools under the superintendence of local authorities remained Protestant schools. Children of all religions were exposed to Protestant proselytizing through the "common" schools.

The Know-Nothing majority was unapologetic: "We teach Protestantism, and believe it to be right, and we glory in that belief."[97]

Public funds also continued to be spent for private schools and academies, all of which incorporated varying degrees of Protestant liturgy into their curriculum.[98] From 1853 to 1917, payments to such schools totaled over $10 million.

Between 1900 and 1910, Catholic immigration to Massachusetts surged, with more than 150,000 Italians, 80,000 Poles, and nearly 25,000 Lithuanians, along with increasing numbers of Jews, Asians, Greeks, Syrians, and others coming to the state. The African American population grew to 14,000 as freed blacks moved north to escape segregation and lynching.[99]

A second generation of nativist groups sprang up, including the American Protective Association, whose members swore never to vote for a Catholic and attempted to restrict immigration to Protestants.

Anti-Catholic sentiment grew as Catholic political power increased and Catholic institutions of higher learning opened. In 1914, David Ignatius Walsh became the Commonwealth's first Irish Catholic governor.

In 1913, the state's Supreme Judicial Court opined that the Anti-Aid Amendment did not prohibit aid to institutions of higher education under sectarian control.[100] In reaction to this ruling, a Constitutional Convention in 1917 modified the Anti-Aid Amendment to prohibit aid to any institution "not publicly owned and under the exclusive control, order and superintendence" of the state or federal government.[101]

Opponents denounced the change as a "gratuitous insult to the Catholic people of this state."[102] However, Catholic legislators viewed it as less offensive than another (more virulent) proposed measure and voted for it out of political expediency. Catholics, one speaker noted, "have paid their share of the nineteen million dollars appropriated to private institutions in the past fifty years," while receiving "comparatively nothing."[103]

Protestant supporters of the amendment said they would "ask no more State aid"[104] and abide by the principle of "equal rights for all, special privileges for none,"[105] but such aid continues to this day. In a typical budget year, grants are made to over 150 private groups, many of them religious. These institutions may perform good works, but the promise of 1917 has been broken. The only institutions not represented on the long list of private beneficiaries of state aid a century later are Catholic schools.[106]

Prejudice against immigrants, and against Catholics in particular, drove the proliferation of similar Anti-Aid or Blaine Amendments in 36 states over six decades. Named for James G. Blaine, the sponsor of a failed amendment to the United States Constitution, these amendments coincided with the development of "common schools" eligible to receive public funds.[107]

Such schools were contrasted with "sectarian" Catholic schools,[108] but the common schools were equally sectarian. They taught doctrine acceptable to Orthodox and Unitarian Congregationalists but offensive to Catholics, Jews, and others.[109]

In Massachusetts, common schools narrowed educational options for those not following the prevailing Protestant orthodoxy, since parents' right to educate their children according to their faith had been protected by the Massachusetts Constitution of 1780. The nativist animus that foreclosed that right in Massachusetts would eliminate competition in American primary and secondary schools across the nation through Blaine Amendments.

Scaling the Higher Wall of Blaine Amendments

The First Amendment to the United States Constitution prohibits both laws that establish government religions and laws that prohibit individuals' free exercise of religion. A state may pass a law that erects a higher wall of separation between church and state, so long as it does not restrict a person's free exercise of religion.

The Massachusetts Supreme Judicial Court has stated that the Anti-Aid Amendment is "more stringent" than the establishment limitations of the First Amendment.[110] Thus, for example, federal cases permit government entities to provide textbooks to parochial school students,[111] while Massachusetts cases do not.[112] Accordingly, Anti-Aid Amendment jurisprudence has developed in a vacuum. The Massachusetts Constitution contains three separate provisions that guarantee religious freedom,[113] but none of them has been invoked in litigation under the Anti-Aid Amendment.

In the federal courts, the bigoted history of Blaine-type limitations on educational diversity was first noted in the 2000 case of *Mitchell v. Helms.*[114] In his plurality opinion, Justice Thomas wrote that:

". . . hostility to aid to pervasively sectarian schools has a shameful pedigree that we do not hesitate to disavow… nothing in the Establishment Clause requires the exclusion of pervasively sectarian schools from otherwise permissible aid programs, and other doctrines of this Court bar it. This doctrine, born of bigotry, should be buried now."[115]

Despite this encouraging sentiment, parents in states with Blaine-type barriers have traditionally faced long odds. The cost of litigation is high, and the long time needed to fully litigate a case can mean a child will have graduated from school before a judicial resolution is obtained.

Supreme Court cases invalidating state constitutional amendments are scarce.[116]

In *Romer v. Evans,*[117] the Supreme Court in 1996 invalidated a state constitutional amendment for the first time on the basis, in part, of animus toward the class of persons affected, namely, homosexuals.[118] A law passed on such a basis does not "bear a rational relationship to a legitimate governmental purpose."[119]

Romer v. Evans concluded that "A law declaring that in general it shall be more difficult for one group of citizens than for all others to seek aid from the government is itself a denial of equal protection in the most literal sense."[120]

The essence of the Anti-Aid Amendment and Blaine Amendments in other states is that certain individuals — parents who wish to educate their children in nongovernment schools — may not seek aid from their state legislatures.

In Massachusetts, the injury is compounded. The same Constitutional Convention that approved the 1917 amendment voted to give the people the right of initiative, but with a unique limitation; it could not be used to repeal either the Anti-Aid Amendment or the provision barring its use to repeal the Anti-Aid Amendment.[121] This double impediment to potential popular repeal or modification violates *Romer v. Evans.*

In 2020, the Supreme Court of the United States took the most important step to date in invalidating most of the Blaine Amendments in state constitutions. In *Espinoza v. Montana Department of Revenue*, the Court held that if a state decides to direct aid to nongovernment institutions, it cannot exclude faith-based institutions from that aid solely because they are faith-based.

The Massachusetts cases that place greater impediments in the way of those seeking aid to educate their children in religious schools than are placed in the way of other citizens are now accordingly subordinate to a U.S. Supreme Court precedent.

What follows is a collection of legal theories and techniques for expanding educational choices.

Substantive Due Process

The doctrine of substantive due process is a restraint, pursuant to the Fourteenth Amendment, on the power of state and federal governments to infringe upon fundamental liberty interests unless the infringement is narrowly tailored to serve a compelling state interest.[122] After a long period of desuetude,[123] the concept of substantive due process made a comeback in the last third of the twentieth century.[124]

In 1925, the Supreme Court, in *Pierce v. Society of Sisters of the Holy Names of Jesus and Mary,* struck down an Oregon state law aimed at immigrants. The Court ruled that the law unreasonably interfered with the "liberty of parents and guardians to direct the upbringing and education of children under their control."[125]

The majority held that "The fundamental theory of liberty upon which all governments in this Union repose excludes any general power of the state to standardize its children by forcing them to accept instruction from public teachers only. The child is not the mere creature of the State."[126]

A substantive due process argument would proceed as follows:

- States with Blaine Amendments tax parents for the support of schools that are inadequate or objectionable.
- The rights of parents in these regards are fundamental.
- There are less intrusive and more effective means to educate children to be informed and self-sufficient citizens.[127]

Such states accordingly have an obligation to provide parents with benefits equivalent to those, received by parents who choose public schools.

Justice Thomas suggested an argument along these lines in his concurring opinion in *Zelman v. Simmons-Harris*, the decision that upheld the Cleveland, Ohio school voucher program. Justice Thomas noted that urban minority children "have been forced into a system that continually fails them,"[128] and called for a more nuanced approach under which state programs of neutral aid would be permitted that did "not impede free exercise rights or any other individual religious liberty interest."[129]

A system of neutral aid to parents would in many cases benefit taxpayers. Annual per-pupil expenditures in fiscal year 2019 were nearly $23,000 in the Boston Public School system, and nearly $30,000 for the Cambridge Public Schools.[130]

By contrast, an inner-city parochial elementary school in Boston charged $5,500 for one child in K2 through Grade 8 and $4,800 for each additional child from a family.[131] Tuitions at representative parochial high schools for 2020–21 include $16,100 at Malden Catholic High School, and $22,950 at Catholic Memorial School in West Roxbury.[132]

The Free Exercise of Religion Clause and the Voucher Model

As noted above, in states with Blaine Amendments, appellate courts have often interpreted such restrictions to be more restrictive than the Establishment Clause of the First Amendment.[133] However, under the Supremacy Clause of the United States Constitution, state constitutional provisions are subordinate to the laws of the United States, including the Free Exercise clause of the First Amendment.

The plaintiffs in *Zelman* did not need to make a First Amendment claim under the Free Exercise Clause, because the Ohio voucher program was in effect and was challenged by state taxpayers on First Amendment Establishment Clause grounds. The decision in *Zelman* is based on the need to provide "educational assistance to poor children in a demonstrably failing public school system"[134] as a "valid secular purpose" sufficient to sustain the law. *Zelman* represented a beginning and not an end.

As the jurisprudence of vouchers has developed, it has proven useful to combine the two types of claims; a secular claim based on the failure of a public education system, and a Free Exercise of Religion claim by one or more parents belonging to a religion whose values are offended by the public school orthodoxy. The plaintiffs' complaint in *Espinoza* rested mainly upon the Free Exercise Clause.

Going Over Blaine's Head

The difficulties faced by parents in states that still have Blaine Amendments on their statute books could be alleviated by direct federal aid to parents in the form of a voucher, or tax relief in the form of a deduction from income or a credit against federal tax liabilities that conformed to the requirements in *Zelman*.

This model is currently in use at the collegiate level, without constitutional objection, through the Pell Grant program. It seems counterintuitive, to say the least, to put direct federal aid in the hands of college freshmen, but not into the hands of parents of elementary and secondary school students who one can reasonably assume will make educational choices from a more mature perspective.

The Contracting Model

State payments to private institutions in Massachusetts can take several forms, including direct grants and amounts paid for services rendered under contracts.[135] The Anti-Aid Amendment bars grants, but not payments for services performed by private educational institutions. Thus, laws authorizing payments to private schools to educate special needs children have been upheld,[136] as have laws requiring local school committees to provide transportation for students attending private schools in fulfillment of compulsory attendance laws.[137]

A practical limitation on the application of these cases is that they involve services ancillary to the function of education itself, namely, transportation, or which affect only a subset of a school's overall student population — special needs children.

In Massachusetts, an extraordinary intervention in the public schools of Chelsea designed to reform that city's chronically underperforming school system survived a challenge under the Anti-Aid Amendment because the Legislature and the governor approved the private institution that was retained to manage the city's schools.[138]

In the absence of special legislation, competition between public and private providers of elementary and secondary education will remain rare. This clashes with a basic principle of good government; namely, that public entities are best served when they can procure goods and services from multiple vendors.[139]

The International Consensus

In recent years, the United States Supreme Court has looked beyond the laws of the United States to the "values we share with a wider civilization" to decide cases involving controversial social issues.[140] It has not yet done so in the realm of parental choice in education, however, even though a parental right to guide a child's free education is included in the United Nations' Declaration of the Rights of the Child,[141] and is recognized in a number of countries.

In France, for example, parochial schools qualify for a variety of subsidies.[142] In the Netherlands, diversity and parental choice result in a large number of children attending both Protestant and Catholic schools at state expense. Until the United States Supreme Court faces the question of whether a parental right to direct a child's compulsory education is limited to the fixed route of the public school to which he or she is consigned by the accidents of birth and wealth, we will not know whether the justices' openness to foreign influences is selective or general.

Conclusion: The Social Benefits of Educational and Religious Diversity

We encourage competition in the marketplace for both public and private services because of the belief, at least as old as Adam Smith, that it produces better results.

"Monopoly," Smith wrote, "is a great enemy to good management, which can never be universally established but in consequence of that free and universal competition which forces everybody to have recourse to it for the sake of self-defence."[143]

We honor this principle in the private sector with antitrust laws, and in the public sector with competitive bidding statutes — except in education.

The existence of alternative school systems supported by parents and religious denominations has served to keep government-funded public schools honest. There is no aspect of K–12 education where the value of this religious diversity is more readily apparent than the sad history of racial segregation in public schools.

Until the 1954 United States Supreme Court decision in *Brown v. Board of Education of Topeka*, the delivery of public education to African Americans was governed by the "separate but equal" doctrine announced in *Plessy v. Ferguson*.[144] The *Brown* decision did not end segregation in America's public schools. Boston's public schools, for example, were not in compliance with *Brown* until 1987.

American Catholic schools integrated much earlier—voluntarily and peacefully—even in urban neighborhoods that were ethnically homogenous and culturally insular. In opposition to the hard-hearted doctrine of "separate but equal," Catholic schools interposed the notion that all children are created in the image and likeness of God.[145]

Religious schools were right about educational segregation in the past; what, in future years, will we discover they've been right about in the present?

The nativist impulse in American public education has often worked to impose pedagogical and religious uniformity upon successive generations, using a government-funded, sole-source provider. Among the principles that have been subordinated to educational uniformity are the right of parents to direct the education of their children, and the right of minorities to receive an adequate education.

The First Amendment's Free Exercise Clause has atrophied, while its Establishment Clause has grown robust; until the two are restored to their intended equilibrium, both parents and children will struggle in the latter's grip.

⁂

Cornelius (Con) Chapman is a lawyer in private practice in Boston who has written on education and public policy topics for Pioneer Institute, Beacon Hill Institute, Reason, *The Boston Herald*, and the Cato Institute. He was the recipient of the 1997 Friend of PACE Award by Parents Alliance for Catholic Education for his *pro bono* work in *Boyette v. Galvin*, which challenged Massachusetts's constitutional provisions that served as a model for Blaine Amendments elsewhere. Chapman is the author of *Rabbit's Blues: The Life and Music of Johnny Hodges* (Oxford University Press), winner of the 2019 Book of the Year Award by *Hot Club de France.*

Chapter 3:
Four Models of Catholic Schooling in Massachusetts

By Cara Stillings Candal, Ed.D.

Introduction

Catholic schools in Massachusetts, including urban ones that have racially and ethnically diverse student bodies with high concentrations of low-income students, outperform their district peers nationwide on achievement tests. Their graduation and college matriculation rates are also higher than their public-school peers,[146] even while per-pupil costs are dramatically less.[147]

Parents — Catholic, non-Catholic, and non-religious — also choose Catholic schools for their safety and a peer culture formed around ethics, morality, duty, and service to others.

Other contributors to this volume have written extensively about the crisis in Catholic schooling in the past 50 years. As fewer men and women choose to become priests and nuns, Catholic schools have hired laypeople to lead and teach in schools, which fundamentally alters how those schools operate. Unlike their predecessors, laypeople require a salary. In response to this important cultural shift and the challenges of a long and difficult sex-abuse scandal that harmed people and (indirectly) schools in Massachusetts and across the world, Catholic leaders and innovators have re-envisioned Catholic education so that it may survive.

Figure 1: Roman Catholic Archdiocese of Boston, 2010 Stanford 10 Results Compared to the National Average[148]

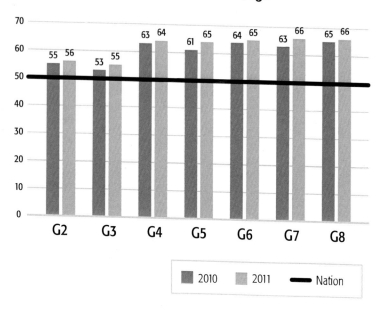

Figure 2: Roman Catholic Archdiocese of Boston, 2010 Stanford 10 Results[149]

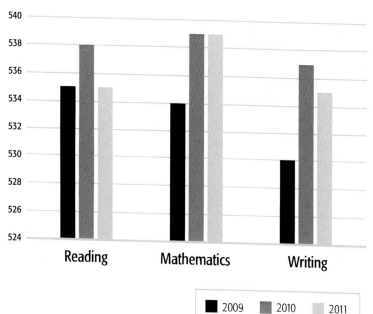

New visions and approaches to Catholic education keep academics and faith at the center but have tweaked or fully changed the financial and governance models. These new models haven't stopped Catholic schools from shuttering across the country, but they have ensured that Catholic school communities in many parts of the state remain able to serve those who desire a Catholic education but may not be able to afford the high cost of private school tuition.

Philanthropy also plays a critical role in the creation of these new models and the perpetuation of Catholic schooling in the Commonwealth more broadly. Catholic schools of the past have always relied upon philanthropy, mainly in the form of support from parishioners who may or may not have used church-affiliated schools.

But as church attendance has declined over time, support has also decreased. Philanthropic organizations have stepped in to fill the void. Unlike individual donors, these organizations operate with specific missions and visions, helping to shape the Catholic schools that they support financially.

Direct scholarships for students are the most common form of support for Catholic schools. A 2014 report from Georgetown University found that 53 percent of parents nationally "identify tuition costs as 'somewhat' or 'very much' a problem when deciding whether to enroll their children in Catholic schools."[150]

The Catholic Schools Foundation is a major Massachusetts philanthropy that grants aid to students to attend schools throughout the Archdiocese of Boston. As of 2020, the Foundation has distributed "more than $100 million in scholarship aid to more than 50,000 students in the greater Boston community."[151]

While direct scholarships are vital, especially for families in urban centers such as Boston, other philanthropies have concentrated on the long-term strategic goal of reinvigorating Catholic education. They have done this by investing in new, more sustainable forms of Catholic education.

The Campaign for Catholic Schools provides an example: Founded in 2010, the Campaign concentrates on revitalizing Catholic education in Boston by building new models of Catholic education that assume lay governance, investing in strong academic programming, teacher, training and technology, and improving facilities. The Campaign has transformed many Catholic schools in the Boston area in the past decade, mainly by forming Catholic "academies" that consolidate and rebuild struggling parish schools.[152]

These investments and others have caused a fundamental shift in the finance and governance models of Catholic schools in some of the Commonwealth's major urban centers. Today, there are distinct "models" of Catholic schooling from which families can choose, and four of those models predominate: Parish schools, academy schools, Cristo Rey schools, and independent Catholic schools.

Linked by a common faith, these four models are distinct enough to provide parents seeking a Catholic education for their children several high-quality options. Most of these models also make Catholic schooling accessible to working and middle-class families.

Parish Schools

Parish schools are not a new model of Catholic education, but those that have survived decades of tumult in Catholic education have done so because they have managed to adapt to changing demographics and the changing needs of families who desire a Catholic education.

Parish schools are pastor-led and tend to be small. They flourished in Boston and nationwide in the 1950s and '60s.[153] As second-generation Irish and Italian families moved from Boston to the suburbs in the 1960s and '70s, suburban parishes and schools formed, although less prolifically than their urban counterparts.[154] Urban parish schools, especially, reflect the changing demographics of the Commonwealth's cities. Schools that once served predominantly Irish and Italian students now serve many more African American and Hispanic students.

Although they are pastor-led, today's parish schools are predominantly staffed by laypeople. The cost of this shift means that many parish schools rely heavily on philanthropy; they fundraise or rely on large donors to provide tuition scholarships for students. As a result, some parish schools may struggle to remain stable or have predictable operational budgets from year to year. If the economy falters and donations to scholarship-granting organizations decline, parish schools suffer.

In the recent decades of declining Catholic school enrollment, parish schools have been the most vulnerable, in part because of their commitment to serving as many families as possible, regardless of ability to pay tuition. When privately funded scholarships or other forms of philanthropy decrease or are spread thin, parish schools will often continue to admit students and operate at a deficit. The short-term decision is rooted in the mission of Catholic education to serve those who need it, but in the long term it is unsustainable and has resulted in mass school closures.

A 2011 article in *The Boston Pilot* on the closure of St. Mary's of the Assumption parish school in Lawrence described how so many parish schools have struggled:

"[T]he kindergarten through grade 8 school is closing because of significant operating deficits... the school is running a $300,000 debt, and more deficits are anticipated as operating costs continue to rise. 'It has also become painfully clear over the past several months that the parish no longer has the fiscal resources to fund the school at the level required,' Father Reyes (head of school) wrote."[155]

Financial problems can also stem from lower demand for parish schools as children grow. Parents tend to seek Catholic education for younger children, in part because children generally receive the sacraments of confirmation and their first Eucharist between pre-kindergarten and grade eight. Thus, parish schools are less abundant at the high school level, which can impact the school decisions that some families make.[156]

And while many parish schools are known for academic rigor and small, tight-knit communities of character, parents may not see them as the best fit for their students as new models of Catholic education become available. Some of these have more and different resources and offerings for students, specifically because they operate with a fundamentally different and more sustainable financial model.

The Academy Model

As parish schools have struggled financially and closed in recent decades, a new model — largely driven by philanthropy — has begun to fill the void. Academy schools are consolidated parish schools; in some cases, up to eight parish schools have consolidated into one academy that can serve more students at scale while preserving low tuitions.

This type of reorganization "provides greater resources for curriculum, staff, technology, and finances and ensures the 'long-term viability' of the schools while maintaining their Catholic identity."[157] Because academy schools can offer additional resources, they may also be more attractive to parents than parish schools, where they still exist.

Like parish schools, academies rely on donors, such as the Catholic Schools Foundation. The difference is that only one entity is "vying for concentrated funding," as opposed to several parishes.[158]

Sister Lucy Veilleux, former principal of Lawrence Catholic Academy, said the academy model "really helps all parish schools involved, relieving them of the individual financial burden."[159]

Other differences between parish schools and academies include governance, size, and school culture. A consolidated school that serves 500 students feels much different than a school that serves 250. The student experience may be less intimate, but the schools have more resources to offer students and teachers, which translates to better outcomes.

For example, Brockton's Trinity Catholic Academy, founded in 2007, provides its students with a high-quality, Catholic alternative to some of the city's district schools. The school serves a high concentration of students who qualify for federal Title I funds, and it reflects the cultural and ethnic diversity of the city of Brockton.

As early as 2013, the school was helping students demonstrate impressive academic growth, "notably in reading and mathematics, with over 90 percent of students showing growth at or above grade level."[160] In 2020, the school boasts that 65 percent of its grade 8 graduates are accepted to competitive Catholic high schools.

How has the school maintained academic excellence? More resources allow school leaders to focus holistically on academics.

"The Academy has made some important decisions about retaining strong teachers and moving weaker teachers out," said Principal Cynthia Dunn McNally. "We have also established some new programs, especially in reading, with a high bar for entrance. We are tracking students, making sure that everything they do is at grade level or above."[161]

Transitioning to a more sustainable academy model did come with growing pains, as beloved parish schools have closed and students and school cultures merge. When Lawrence Catholic Academy was born of the merger of several surrounding parish schools, Sister Veilleux said, the difficulties included making sure that one school's culture or faculty didn't become too dominant, and that the new school maintained a distinctly Catholic brand of education. Fortunately, the merged schools all had similar academic standards and expectations.[162]

A decade after that merger, Lawrence Catholic Academy has become its own school with its own distinct character, rooted in the Catholic faith. It has also managed to survive some of the very daunting economic challenges the decade has brought, in large part because it represents this new, more sustainable model of Catholic education.

Cristo Rey

Massachusetts is home to two schools in the national Cristo Rey Network, bringing a college preparatory education to children from families of limited means. The first Cristo Rey Jesuit High School opened in Chicago in 1996, with a model that combines high-quality education with a work-study program."[163]

Massachusetts Cristo Rey students work five full days each month in "some of the best-known companies in the state, building résumés, contacts, and experience that will have an immeasurable impact on their lives."[164] Students contribute to their tuition, learning work and life skills."[165]

Cristo Rey schools can be sponsored by different religious orders and have their own governance structure, but each agrees to serve only disadvantaged students, to require workstudy, and to be explicitly Catholic.[166]

Cristo Rey Boston (now in Dorchester) began in a once-thriving parish school in Cambridge, whose leaders turned to the Cristo Rey Network and reopened the school as Cambridge Catholic High School in 2004.[167]

Though it is independently governed, Cristo Rey Boston is affiliated with the Archdiocese. Cardinal Sean O'Malley is the signatory on the school's agreement with the Cristo Rey Network, the Archdiocese appoints board members, and the school leases its building from the Archdiocese for $1 annually.[168]

At Cristo Rey Boston, only 10 percent of funding is generated by tuitions, while 70 percent comes from work-study and 20 percent from outside donors, including non-Catholic ones.[169]

Notre Dame High School in Lawrence, which also opened in 2004, is run by the Sisters of Notre Dame de Namur. The order's mission—"to stand with poor people, especially women and children, in the most abandoned places"—is well aligned with the Cristo Rey mission.[170]

Both Notre Dame High School and Cristo Rey fill a void in the Catholic school landscape, remaining open and virtually tuition-free thanks to their work-study program. They continue the Catholic school tradition of finding a way to close the gap between those with resources and those without.

Rigorous academics, Advanced Placement (AP) courses,[171] and a safe environment where all students feel welcome and challenged contribute to the popularity of the Cristo Rey model. Cristo Rey schools are college preparatory environments.

"I think they want us to have a better future for us, and for our next generation as well," one student said. "They want us to go to college."[172]

Figure 3: Selected student demographics, Cristo Rey Boston. Footnote: Information from Cristo Rey Boston, 2017 Annual Report[173]

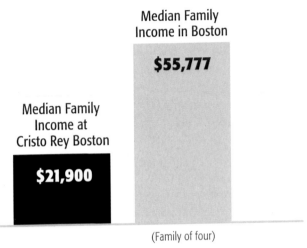

Median Family Income in Boston

$55,777

Median Family Income at Cristo Rey Boston

$21,900

(Family of four)

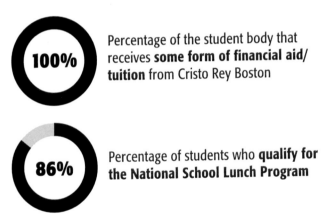

100% Percentage of the student body that receives **some form of financial aid/tuition** from Cristo Rey Boston

86% Percentage of students who **qualify for the National School Lunch Program**

Catholic and non-Catholic students see Cristo Rey schools as a desirable alternative to both district public schools and even high-performing charter public schools. In 2019, 100 percent of graduates from Cristo Rey Boston were accepted to college.[174] This is much higher than the national average of about 62 percent.[175]

Independent Catholic Schools

The fourth model of Catholic schooling, independent schools, are operated by entities other than the Archdiocese. Independent Catholic schools can be diverse in mission and vision, and their "independence" refers more to the model of governance than a financial, curricular, or pedagogical model.

In Massachusetts, some independent Catholic schools are considered elite because of competitive admissions processes and sometimes very high tuitions. In these ways, independent schools are different than other Catholic school models.[176]

Figure 4: Cristo Rey Boston SAT, Compared to Top-Performing Boston Schools[177]

Rank	School	Math	Writing
1	Boston Latin	638	613
2	Boston Latin Academy	548	528
3	Boston Collegiate	504	480
4	O'Bryant Public School	523	457
5	Academy of Pacific Rim	489	470
6	**Cristo Rey Academy**	**480**	**471**
7	MATCH	492	434
8	Another Course to College	439	437
9	Fenway School	431	427
10	City on a Hill	446	416

Independent Catholic schools have a long tradition. Some of the best-known, including Boston College High and Ursuline Academy, are independently governed, although subject to the ultimate authority of the bishop, who must approve each school's official Catholic program and religion classes. Fully independent boards have authority for all other decision-making. Independent schools may be affiliated with a religious order but are not affiliated with a parish or pastor.[178]

Independent Catholic schools were not always considered elite, and they weren't always so expensive. Boston College High School, located in Dorchester, has undergone significant change. According to Stephen Hughes, former headmaster:

"For a long time, Boston College High School educated the sons of immigrants. It was established in response to the anti-Catholicism at the turn of the century and the notion that education was part of a cradle-to-grave Catholicism. This school was established to prepare boys to go on to further Catholic education and be Catholic citizens."[179]

Today, Boston College High School, a school that is rooted in a long Jesuit tradition (although no longer officially run by the Society of Jesus), is a rigorous exam school that turns away three or four students for every one it takes. Students come from Boston, its suburbs, and even New Hampshire because the education they receive is rooted in Catholic tradition, confers ideals of service to others, and provides entry into the country's top colleges.

"We form young men that have a conscience and will act on that," said Hughes. "Conscience should permeate everything we do: science, language, math, history... We believe in developing a morality (in our students) that says you have to change the structural things that keep injustice alive."[180]

This commitment to altering injustice through education comes in two forms at Boston College High School. First, all students are required to perform community service. Second, the school earmarks a great deal of money for financial aid to enable needy students to attend. About 18 percent of young boys at Boston College High School are considered low-income.[181]

Ursuline Academy in Dedham is another competitive independent Catholic school that has also served a population of students less racially and culturally diverse than many parish and academy Catholic schools. An all-women's school, Ursuline Academy is known for academics as rigorous as those at Boston College High School. Students are admitted based on exam scores and recommendations of their math and English abilities. They also have access to AP courses and an array of extracurriculars.[182]

These two competitive and comparatively expensive examples, although well-known in Massachusetts, do not represent all independent schools in the Commonwealth. Cathedral High School of Boston, for example, provides a rigorous Catholic education at a very low cost (comparatively) of $7,000 per student. The school does this by raising philanthropy to bridge the gap between the $20,000 it actually invests in each student and the cost of tuition. This model allows Cathedral to serve students from the South End of Boston, where it is located, and surrounding communities, providing those who attended urban elementary schools in the area with an affordable and continuous Catholic education.

Summary and Recommendations for Change

For decades, Catholic schools have served students and families regardless of background or income, enabling even the most disadvantaged students to succeed academically and go on to college. But as the Catholic Church has struggled, so has its schools. Fortunately, new innovations in Catholic schooling have been born of that struggle and a persisting will to serve anyone who desires a high-quality Catholic education, regardless of background.

The four models of Catholic schooling outlined here represent important vestiges of traditional governance and operating approaches to Catholic schooling. They also represent a new chapter in Catholic education, even as 2020 has brought new challenges to all private schools, especially those that serve lower-income students.

If Catholic schools as a group are to survive and grow, they should continue to envision new approaches to governance and funding. Advocates, especially in Massachusetts, should also focus on new opportunities.

Specifically, the 2020 U.S. Supreme Court decision in *Espinoza v. Montana Department of Revenue* has pointed out the bigoted roots of the Commonwealth's Anti-Aid Amendments, and the opportunity to enact state-sponsored tuition-tax credits — or even a new approach to school funding that would allow students to take state funds to schools of choice, whether those schools are public or private, faith-based or secular.

Recommendations

Be transparent about the successes and challenges of the tradition models of Catholic education

Catholic schools have a long tradition of helping the neediest students achieve academic success, yet not all schools collect and publish data that can help the public understand the outcomes they achieve. Doing so could help families and politicians understand why and how to support them. This recommendation could be achieved with assistance from a central body, such as the Catholic school offices in the archdioceses of the Commonwealth. Greater clarity and transparency in the collection and use of data could unite autonomous schools across what is a great system.

Pursue innovative funding and governance models

Cristo Rey Network schools in Massachusetts adhere to an innovative funding model that works. While they rely on some outside funding, they attract a much broader donor base because donors know and like the Cristo Rey work-study program, which has attracted valuable, national attention for students. The academy model, too, is an innovation born of necessity. By consolidating struggling schools, academies have not only kept Catholic schools operating for the students who want them, they have created a scale that allows for better, more concentrated resources.

Promote tuition tax credits (and more)

Tuition tax credits for Massachusetts families will make a high-quality Catholic education available to more children and help ease the fundraising burden on Catholic schools. Tax credits could enable Catholic schools to charge tuition in line with actual per-pupil costs and thus better address many of the issues raised in this chapter, including teacher retention, by enabling more of these schools to pay teachers a living wage.

States across the country can provide an example for Massachusetts. Currently, there are 25 voucher programs and 22 tax-credit programs in 26 states, all of which provide students with the opportunity to attend private schools, including Catholic schools, at no cost.

In the wake of the 2020 *Espinoza* decision and very strong evidence that private school choice programs help both students who use them and those who remain in public schools, Massachusetts should consider a new approach to supporting the education of all children.[183]

Support school models that provide distinctive opportunities and academic quality

Creation of the academy and Cristo Rey models of Catholic education in particular represent true innovations in school finance and governance. By consolidating parish schools, academies have managed to operate with more sustainable budgets than their parish school predecessors, without sacrificing low tuitions or academic quality. The Cristo Rey model provides unique opportunities for older students while not relying solely on philanthropy, which is also a key to sustainability. Leaders in Catholic education should consider how to grow these and similar models with an eye to what financial stability and scale allow school leaders to do — invest in talent, high-quality curricula, technology, and family support.

Cara Stillings Candal, Ed.D., has spent the last 10 years working in education policy as a Senior Fellow with both Pioneer Institute and the Center for Education Reform. She was also a founding team member of the National Academy of Advanced Teacher Education (NAATE) and a research assistant professor at Boston University in the Department of Educational Leadership and Development. Candal has authored/edited more than 25 papers and three books on education policy. She earned a Bachelor of Arts in English Literature from Indiana University, a Master of Arts in Social Science from the University of Chicago, and a Doctor of Education from Boston University. Candal is the author most recently of Pioneer Institute's book, *The Fight for the Best Charter Public Schools in the Nation*.

Chapter 4:
Giving Kids Credit: Using Scholarship Tax Credits to Increase Educational Opportunity in Massachusetts

By Ken Ardon, Ph.D., Jason Bedrick & Martin F. Lueken, Ph.D.

Introduction

Education and Equality of Opportunity

Massachusetts consistently ranks among the very top performers on the National Assessment of Educational Progress (NAEP), which is commonly referred to as "the nation's report card,"[184] and is internationally competitive in math and science according to Trends in International Mathematics and Science Study (TIMSS) and Programme for International Student Assessment (PISA) testing.[185] However, these aggregate scores obscure the reality that performance varies considerably across districts, particularly along socioeconomic lines.

In wealthier municipalities such as Dover and Weston, with higher median household incomes, students perform well.[186] By contrast, students from lower-income communities such as Lawrence and New Bedford, where the median household income is much lower, are more likely to struggle to reach proficiency. This pattern is repeated across the Commonwealth—low-income, black, and Hispanic students in poorer districts consistently struggle to achieve proficiency at the same rates as their counterparts in wealthier districts.[187]

Wealthier families already have educational choice. They can afford to live in communities with higher-performing schools or send their children to private schools. Since they have the ability to exit, the public schools must be responsive to their children's needs. Lower-income families often have only one viable option: the public school to which their children are assigned. Some may have charter schools in their community, but the number of seats is limited. Most low-income parents are a captive audience, so their schools become de facto monopolies.

Education Choice and the "Know-Nothing" Amendments

While educational choice programs are not a panacea, they are a precondition to ensuring equality of opportunity. Yet efforts to expand educational opportunity face a significant legal obstacle: the "Know-Nothing" amendments to the Massachusetts Constitution.

As discussed in Chapter 2, the nativist and anti-Catholic "Know-Nothing" party succeeded in amending the Massachusetts Constitution in 1855 to block the Commonwealth from supporting Catholic schools, though at the time the state-supported common schools were *de facto* non-denominational Protestant, and many continued to receive public funding.

A 1917 constitutional convention amended the 1855 provision so as to bar public money for any school "...wherein any denominational doctrine is inculcated, or any other school, or any college ... or educational, charitable or religious undertaking which is not publicly owned and under the exclusive control, order and superintendence of public officers or public agents authorized by the commonwealth or federal authority or both..."[188]

Under this provision, it would likely be unconstitutional for Massachusetts to enact a publicly funded school voucher program that included religiously affiliated schools, although it's possible that excluding such schools would violate the Free Exercise Clause of the First Amendment. Moreover, the Supreme Court's 2020 decision in *Espinoza v. Montana Department of Revenue* could push the Commonwealth closer to a voucher-like program over time.[189]

Until that happens, proponents of educational choice may still have a constitutionally viable option. A tax-credit scholarship (TCS) program lets private individuals and corporations receive a tax credit for donating to private, nonprofit organizations that grant scholarships to children of low-income families to use at nonpublic schools, out-of-district public schools, or for certain homeschooling expenses.

The United States Supreme Court ruled in *ACSTO v. Winn* (2011) that private money does not become public money until it has "come into the tax collector's hands."[190]

Likewise, the Arizona Supreme Court ruled that a TCS program did not violate Arizona's "No-Aid" amendment, which is similar to Massachusetts' Know-Nothing Amendments, because it did not entail the expenditure of public money.[191]

Massachusetts already allows religiously affiliated schools and houses of worship to benefit from tax breaks that serve a secular purpose and are neutral with respect to religion. Likewise, a tax-credit scholarship program serves the secular purpose of expanding educational opportunities and is neutral with respect to religion since parents can choose among educational options.

Tax-Credit Scholarship Programs in the United States

There are currently more than 300,000 students receiving scholarships through 23 tax-credit scholarship programs operating in 18 states, including Alabama, Arizona, Florida, Georgia, Illinois, Indiana, Iowa, Kansas, Louisiana, Montana, Nevada, New Hampshire, Oklahoma, Pennsylvania, Rhode Island, South Carolina, South Dakota, and Virginia.[192] Additionally, Utah enacted the nation's 24th tax-credit scholarship policy for students with special needs in 2020.[193]

At their core, the TCS programs are very similar. Taxpayers receive tax credits for contributions to scholarship organizations that fund students attending schools other than their assigned public school.

Almost all existing programs require that the household income of would-be scholarship recipients fall below a certain threshold. Some programs are limited to students with special needs, students who previously attended a public school, or students who would be assigned to a failing public school. Scholarship recipients in some states can only redeem the scholarships at private schools, while recipients in other states may attend out-of-district public schools.

This chapter discusses the implications of these policy decisions and proposes a model scholarship tax credit program for Massachusetts.

Research on Educational Choice

Effect on Participating Student Outcomes

Educational choice programs are among the most studied education policy interventions, and the consensus of high-quality research is that choice and competition improve educational outcomes.

Random-assignment studies are the gold standard of social science research because they compare two groups that are different only due to the "treatment" (in this case, receiving a scholarship to attend a nonpublic school) and random chance.

In 2020, researchers conducted a literature review of existing high-quality studies of private school choice program outcomes.[194] EdChoice reviewed 17 random assignment studies of private school choice program effects on academic outcomes and educational attainment.

Of the 17 studies, 11 found that educational choice programs had a positive impact on the standardized test scores of participating students, either for the full sample or for subgroups (such as low-income students). Four found no visible effects. Only three studies found a negative impact on student outcomes; two of these evaluated Louisiana's voucher program, which researchers believe was hobbled by poor implementation and overregulation.[195] One study of Milwaukee's voucher program found both positive and negative effects.

Additionally, four out of six studies found that educational choice programs had a positive effect on participating students' likelihood of graduating high school and attending college. Two studies found no visible impact, and none found a negative impact.

In 2009, Andrew J. Coulson of the Cato Institute published a global literature review that analyzed more than 150 statistical comparisons covering eight educational outcomes. They ranged from more market-like systems to those with more centralized government control. The review concluded that it is "the least regulated market school systems that show the greatest margin of superiority over state schooling"[196]—higher student achievement, greater parental satisfaction, and higher average attainment levels.

Parental Satisfaction

Parents consistently report very high levels of satisfaction with the schools they select for their children through educational choice programs. National data from 2019 show that parents are more likely to report being satisfied with a school, whether public or private, if it is a school of choice. Parents who choose private schools are much more likely to report being satisfied.[197]

Surveys of tax-credit programs, specifically, support these findings. A 2018 survey of the nation's largest tax-credit scholarship program, the Florida Tax Credit Scholarship, found that "92 percent of parents expressed satisfaction with the program, including 89 percent who were 'completely satisfied.'"[198]

Parents who live in states with smaller tax-credit programs that serve fewer pupils express similarly high satisfaction rates. A 2014 study of New Hampshire's tax-credit scholarships found that 97 percent of respondents were satisfied, with 89.5 percent "very satisfied."[199]

Effects of Competition on Public School Performance

The benefits of educational choice programs are not confined to participating students. Public school students can also benefit, because choice programs create an incentive for schools to compete for students. When parents can vote with their feet, schools must work hard to meet children's needs. The above-mentioned literature review reported that 25 of 27 empirical studies found that educational choice programs improve academic outcomes at public schools.[200]

One of these studies measured the impact of the threat of competition from Florida's scholarship tax credit program.[201] Since state funding of public schools is tied to enrollment, public schools lose money for each student who chooses to leave for another school, thereby creating an incentive to compete. The study utilized four measures of competition: the *distance* to the nearest private school, the *density* of private schools within a five-mile radius, the *diversity* of private schools in that area, and the *concentration* of different types of private schools in the area.

The study concluded that "all four measures of competition — distance, density, diversity, and concentration — are positively related to student performance on state math and reading tests."[202]

Fiscal Impact of TCS Programs

The fiscal impact of a tax-credit scholarship program depends upon its design and how the state funds public education. Where funding is tied to enrollment, well-designed TCS programs produce savings for state taxpayers when the reduction in state expenditures from students switching to private schools exceeds tax credit disbursements given to taxpayers for donations to scholarship organizations. Factors that influence the fiscal impact of these programs include the size of the credit and amount of tax credit disbursements, average scholarship size, number of switchers, and the percentage of scholarship students who qualify for additional state aid (including federal free and reduced lunch, English language learners, and students with disabilities).

Among existing TCS programs, tax credit rates range from 50 percent to 100 percent of donations to scholarship organizations. All else being equal, lower tax credit rates produce greater savings, but higher tax credits induce taxpayers to contribute more, allowing for far more students to receive scholarships.

Policy makers must balance the goals of saving money and aiding the greatest number of students. Many TCS programs cap the total or average scholarship size at a figure that is considerably less than the state's average per-pupil expenditure. A lower average scholarship size will produce greater savings, but the neediest families require larger scholarships to allow them to afford the school of their choice. Most programs also place limits on the total amount of tax credits available for disbursement. The downside is that such caps may limit student participation in the program (perhaps below a desired level of participation), lower the value of scholarships, and limit the level of financial assistance provided for individual families, or both.

States only save money when a student switches from a public school to a private or home school or when scholarships are provided to students who would otherwise attend a public school without financial assistance from an educational choice program. In many TCS programs, students are only eligible for scholarships if they attended a public school in the previous year or, in some cases, are entering kindergarten or first grade.[203]

Researchers have conducted random assignment studies of several private school choice programs and report information that can help infer switcher rates. When a student applies to an oversubscribed program and loses a lottery, researchers observe the type of school that student returns to. Switcher rates among private school choice programs tend to be quite high—lower-bound and upper-bound weighted average switcher rates are 84 percent and 90 percent.[204] Most students participating in private school choice programs are generating savings that more than offset total program costs and result in net fiscal benefits.

A study of 10 TCS programs in seven states estimated that these programs generated positive net fiscal benefits for state and local taxpayers worth between $1,650 and $3,000 per scholarship student through FY 2014.[205] The fiscal effects from these programs represent cumulative savings for state and local taxpayers combined worth between $1.7 billion and $3.4 billion.

Researchers have also calculated the fiscal impact of the three longest running and largest TCS programs. A 2009 study estimated that Arizona's TCS program saved state taxpayers between $100 million and $242 million during calendar year 2008.[206] A 2011 study of the Earned Income Tax Credit (EITC) program in Pennsylvania estimated that the program saved the state and districts about $512 million each year while reducing state tax revenue by only about $40 million.[207] Another fiscal analysis examined the EITC and Opportunity Scholarship Tax Credit (OSTC) programs in Pennsylvania. It estimated that between FY 2002 and FY 2019 the EITC and OSTC programs generated between $3 billion and $5 billion in cumulative net fiscal benefits for state and local taxpayers combined, or up to $6,800 per scholarship.[208]

In 2010, the Florida Legislature's nonpartisan Office of Program Policy Analysis and Government Accountability estimated that Florida's TCS program saved the state $32.6 million ($1.44 in savings for each dollar tax credit).[209] The scholarships are intended to make up the difference between what the families can afford and the schools' own need-based tuition breaks. The poorest families often have only small copayments.

Thirteen of the 24 TCS programs currently in operation, including Florida's, offer full tax credits (100 percent rate, or one dollar of tax credits disbursed for each dollar donated to a TCS program).[210] Eleven TCS programs offer partial credits, as low as 50 percent in Indiana and Oklahoma, though most partial credits are between 75 percent and 90 percent.

On a per-student basis, average funding of TCS programs is about $3,800. This public cost represents 37 percent of the total public per-student cost to educate TCS student in public schools.[211] This large funding disparity suggests that fiscal benefits accrue to taxpayers. How these benefits are distributed and to whom poses a more complex question. Below, we discuss the potential fiscal effects of TCS programs on state taxpayers and public school districts.

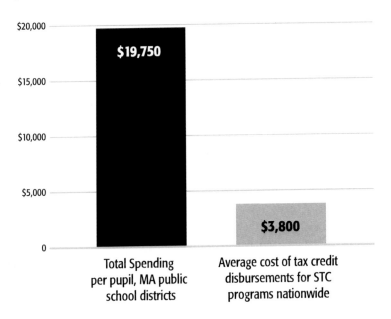

Fiscal Impact of a TCS Program in Massachusetts

A tax-credit program scholarship produces both foregone state tax revenue due to tax credit disbursements and a decline in state and local education spending due to students leaving the public schools.[212] The revenue side is straightforward — the state forgoes some revenue by disbursing tax credits to taxpayers for donations to scholarship organizations. The impact on state spending for the K–12 public school system is more complex and depends on the school funding formula and the design of the TCS program. The program's fiscal impact depends on the generosity of the tax credits and scholarships, the number of students leaving public schools, student backgrounds and educational needs, and the geographic distribution of the recipients.

School Funding in Massachusetts

In FY 2018, total per-pupil expenditures for Massachusetts public school districts was $19,750.[213] School districts receive revenue from three sources: federal, state, and local governments, comprising 5 percent, 38 percent, and 57 percent of total revenue, respectively.[214] Because a significant portion of the per-pupil funds is not directly determined by students, not every dollar of that student's per-pupil funding follows a student when they enter or leave a school district of their choosing.[215]

This arrangement for K–12 public schools differs dramatically from other enterprises in American society (e.g., higher education, pre-K, health care, retail) where every dollar follows a student, client, patient, or customer when they switch from one service provider to another. Thus, when students leave a public school district, students who remain in the district end up with more resources on a per-student basis, all other things being equal.

School funding in Massachusetts is determined by a complex formula called Chapter 70. The funding formula begins with the calculation of the foundation budget, which estimates the per-pupil cost to provide teachers, materials, and other resources to provide an adequate education. The foundation budget varies depending on whether a child attends a vocational school, speaks English, is from a low-income household, and whether the school they attend is an elementary, middle or high school. The foundation budget represents the absolute minimum a district is required to spend, although most school districts are required to spend more than the foundation.[216]

The last part of the formula calculates state aid, beginning with the prior year's aid and then considering two main adjustments. Districts receive foundation aid if the combination of the required local contribution plus the prior year's aid is not enough to reach foundation. Foundation aid is usually greater in lower-income districts. Second, the Commonwealth calculates target aid, a percentage of the foundation budget it will fund based on each municipality's property wealth and income.[217]

How a TCS Program Impacts School Funding in Massachusetts

The net fiscal impact of an educational choice program is simply the savings incurred from students redirected from public schools (referred to as switchers throughout this chapter) minus the cost of the TCS program:

Net fiscal impact = [Savings from student switchers] – [Total public cost for TCS]

A tax-credit scholarship program would reduce the number of students in some public schools, with a complex impact on local school contributions. In communities with required contributions above their target share, a TCS program would reduce the required local contribution as enrollment and the foundation budget decline. It is impossible to determine how many of these communities would reduce their actual local spending as the required local contribution fell. For the majority of communities, a TCS program would have no impact on the required local contribution because local effort is determined by property wealth and residents' incomes rather than enrollment or the foundation budget.[218]

However, nearly all municipalities choose to spend more than required.[219] Reductions in enrollment — and in state aid — could lead these cities and towns to change their spending even though the required local contribution does not change.

Given that state funding has a more direct link to student enrollment and background than other funding sources, a scholarship program would have a much clearer impact on state aid.[220] When students choose to leave a district school via an educational choice program (or for any other reason), the district's foundation budget will be reduced. This reduction, in turn, translates into savings for state taxpayers which offset the TCS program's cost. The reduction in the state's payments for state aid may partially or completely offset the cost of the program. If the reduction in state aid exceeds the TCS program's cost, then the TCS program generates a net fiscal benefit for state taxpayers.

The actual impact on state aid varies across districts and depends primarily on whether the district is a foundation aid district (i.e., a district that requires additional foundation aid when the foundation budget increases) and how much aid would have changed had the students not left.[221]

State Impact in Foundation and Above-Foundation Districts

In foundation aid districts, a drop in enrollment and the foundation budget has a direct impact on state aid. These districts tend to be low-income and urban. If a student leaves the district, the district's foundation budget would fall by about $12,000 on average, and the district would require $12,000 less aid to reach foundation.[222] Some students, such as special needs students, students from low-income families, and English language learners, generate additional foundation funding for school districts.

Let's consider a foundation aid district with 5,000 students, 1 percent of whom (50 students) choose to participate in an TCS program. We assume funding for the foundation budget at $12,000 per student. This shift would reduce the district's foundation budget by $12,000 per student (or $600,000) and state aid by the same amount. Thus, the state would experience $600,000 in reduced payments to the district. Say the state awards $200,000 in tax credits to incentivize giving for scholarship organizations to provide students with scholarships (an average cost of $4,000, which is slightly above the average cost of all currently existing TCS programs). Then the state's net fiscal impact would be $400,000 in net savings due to the program.

By contrast, in an above-foundation district, a decrease in student enrollment would have a more limited impact on state taxpayers. If a district's target share for state aid is 40 percent of foundation, the district could require $4,800 less aid per student (40 percent of $12,000). If 50 students leave to participate in a TCS program, the district would see state aid reduced by about $240,000. The state would incur $240,000 in savings to offset its cost to support these students in the TCS program. The state's net fiscal impact would be $40,000 in this example.

The example above represents an upper limit on state aid reduction. The reduction in state aid for above-foundation districts could be less for a couple of reasons. First, target aid has never been fully funded, which effectively postpones some of the savings to the state from an STC program. Second, some districts are above both foundation and their target share. In these districts, the loss of students would not have any substantial impact on state aid. In general, the largest impact is in foundation aid districts, with the smaller impact in other districts dependent on income and property values.

Does a Drop in Enrollment Actually Decrease Aid? Massachusetts's Hold Harmless Funding

In principle, districts with flat or declining enrollment could receive less state aid. However, historically the state has almost never reduced state aid to districts. The state's "hold harmless" funding provision ensures that state aid generally does not decline for school districts.[223] That is, a district is guaranteed at least the same level of state aid it received the prior year *plus* an additional $30 per student, regardless of its present year's enrollment or student needs.[224] This funding mechanism serves as a one-way funding ratchet for districts. It also means that the distribution of fiscal effects will be uneven between the state and school districts as well as across districts.

The hold harmless provision will reduce the amount the state saves, but it is difficult to model the exact impact because it depends on the number of students leaving each district. Compared to a world without hold harmless in place, state taxpayers will realize fewer savings from students participating in the program while districts will disproportionately enjoy greater fiscal benefits. And districts with greater reliance on state aid will disproportionately benefit by receiving more hold harmless funding relative to districts that receive less state aid.

The rationale for maintaining aid when enrollment declines

is that schools face fixed costs that do not change when the number of students changes. However, an analysis by the Friedman Foundation (now EdChoice) estimated that 73.3 percent of per-pupil costs in Massachusetts are short-run variable costs.[225] Given this economic reality and increasingly high cost of this particular funding mechanism, it would be fiscally prudent for the Commonwealth to revisit the hold harmless policy. If the state aid formula is not adjusted, reductions in enrollment could lead to ever higher levels of state aid per pupil that are unrelated to the costs of educating students.

Fiscal Impact on School Districts

As described above, a TCS program would reduce state aid and, to a lesser extent, the required local contribution from municipalities by a student's foundation amount when that student chooses to leave a district to participate in the TCS program. The amount of this reduction is, on average, $12,000 per student. While districts would receive less state aid and potentially less local funding, they would also have fewer students and lower educational costs.[226] A hypothetical example illustrates the potential of a TCS program on a district that allowed 50 students to transfer to private school.

A reduction in student enrollment will reduce educational costs in the short run for school districts. Using methods more cautious than Scafidi's (2012) already cautious approach, we estimate that 70 percent of total expenditures are variable in the short run (i.e., costs that change directly with enrollment).[227] On a per-student basis, average short-run variable costs for Massachusetts public schools is about $13,800 per student. Thus, on average, Massachusetts school districts have about $13,800 in variable cost savings to offset their state aid reduction.

For example, if 50 students leave for any reason, a district's short-run costs, on average, will be reduced by about $690,000. For an above-foundation aid district, this enrollment shift would imply a reduction in state aid up to $600,000. Because of hold harmless, state aid that flows to a district will be wholly or partially protected, i.e., the district keeps all or a portion of state aid funds. As a result, in addition to avoiding some reduction in Chapter 70 funding, the district's educational costs decrease by $690,000 in the short run. The district ends up with significantly more resources for fewer students than it otherwise would have had without hold harmless.

Now let's consider an above-foundation aid district whose state share is 40 percent. If 50 students leave, the district's total revenue reduction will be $600,000. Of this reduction, $240,000 reflects state aid and the remainder consists of a decrease in local effort. Under hold harmless, however, state aid is partially protected, and the district retains up to $240,000 in state aid. Its net Chapter 70 revenue reduction is $360,000. The district's educational costs decrease by $690,000 in the short run. This variable cost burden relief significantly exceeds the district's $360,000 reduction in Chapter 70 revenue. The district also ends up with significantly more resources for fewer students than it otherwise would have had without hold harmless. Even if the district chooses to reduce costs commensurate with its Chapter 70 revenue reduction ($360,000), students who remain in the district still end up with more resources ($331,000 worth).

To be sure, given the significant funding gaps between public school systems and school choice programs, a common byproduct of choice programs is that affected districts typically experience growth in per-pupil spending, even in states without hold harmless provisions.

Unequal Fiscal Impact

The impact of a TCS program would vary by district. The logic of the changes in state aid is clear: If students do not attend a district, the district should not receive state aid. However, because the state aid formula is moderately progressive and provides larger amounts of aid to poorer districts, those districts would lose more aid per pupil when students left.

Since the TCS program is targeted toward low-income students, districts with higher concentrations of low-income families are likely to lose more students than richer districts. As students leave public schools, the districts forgo the aid associated with those students, so lower-income districts will be more affected than higher-income districts—many of which would not lose any aid even if they lost students.

It is easy to misinterpret or overstate the importance of this disparate impact. First, the reason higher-income districts see little or no reduction in aid is that they would not have received an increase in aid if the student attended the district. Second, the reductions in aid refer to the aggregate aid, but enrollment is also falling; the net effect is to increase spending per pupil. Finally, the "reductions" in aid discussed here would occur in a world without the state's hold harmless funding provision in place; because of hold harmless, no districts actually lose aid.

It is important to recognize that the impact of a TCS on school finances is exactly the same as if a student graduated or moved out of the district, or a child enrolled in private or home school.

The ultimate fiscal impact of a TCS program on local districts is likely to be small—budgets would only grow more slowly than they would have, and districts that lose the most aid would also be the ones losing the most students, so that spending per pupil rises. And, as discussed earlier, the overwhelming consensus of research demonstrates that districts respond in positive ways when states expand educational opportunity for their families and increase competition.

How a Model TCS Program Could Work

Policy makers must balance competing considerations when crafting a tax-credit scholarship program. This proposal is tailored for Massachusetts and aims to aid as many low-income families as possible while reducing state expenditures as much or more than the concurrent loss in state revenue.

Eligibility

We propose setting eligibility to receive a scholarship at 250 percent of federal poverty line, which was $65,500 for a family of four in 2020.[228]

Almost all existing TCS programs have a means-testing provision, and of those all but Pennsylvania's peg their income threshold to the federal poverty line (FPL) or the federal Free and Reduced Lunch program. The FPL guidelines are already used for numerous state and federal programs, are adjusted annually, and consider family size. As discussed below, this measure would ensure greater savings due to Massachusetts's funding formula.

Tax Credit Value

We propose a tax credit worth 90 percent of taxpayer donations to scholarship organizations. To maximize the number of students the TCS program can aid, the credit amount should be as high as possible while still producing fiscal savings. A smaller credit could hurt fundraising, but previous research has indicated that setting the tax credit amount at this level would not significantly impact the fundraising efforts of scholarship organizations.[229]

Average Scholarship Cap

As discussed above, a cap on the average scholarship amount rather than the total amount gives scholarship organizations greater flexibility to tailor scholarships to the financial situation of individual families. The scholarships are intended to bridge the gap between what families can afford and the cost of tuition; therefore, the average scholarship cap should be as high as possible without sacrificing fiscal savings.

Based on the estimates discussed below, we propose an average scholarship cap starting at $4,500 per student and rising with inflation.

According to Private School Review, the median tuition for private elementary schools in Massachusetts was $12,983 during the 2018–19 school year.[230] However, the tuition that most low-income students face is much lower. In the five lowest-income cities among the Commonwealth's 10 most populous cities—Springfield, Fall River, New Bedford, Brockton, and Lynn—the median tuition was $4,470 for kindergarten, $4,173 for grades 1–5, $4,510 for grades 6–8, and $9,125 for high school. Moreover, these figures do not include the tuition aid that such schools offer low-income families. The proposed scholarship amount would likely cover a significant portion of tuition at many schools.

Total Credit Cap

Total credit caps are often imposed to limit the impact of the program on public school funding, since states like Massachusetts provide funding to public schools based in part on enrollment. If enough families accept scholarships and leave the public school system, the budgets of some public schools have the potential to decline. If lawmakers decide to impose a total credit cap, the scholarship program should include an escalator provision that automatically raises the cap over time.

Scholarship programs without an escalator often remain stuck at the same maximum funding level for several years, despite growing demand and the fact that the real value of the scholarships diminishes over time due to inflation.[231]

Fiscal Impact of the Proposed TCS Program

What is the fiscal impact of a TCS program as described above? The design of a TCS program, including the number of low-income recipients, the amount of the scholarships, and the percentage of the tax credit, would determine the fiscal impact on the Commonwealth. However, the consequences also depend upon the geographic distribution of scholarship recipients and the share of recipients who would not have attended public schools.

The first element can be modeled based on existing data. For example, low-income scholarship recipients are more likely to come from districts with more low-income students. Statistics on household income around Massachusetts are not a perfect predictor of the number of students who would receive scholarships. Other factors such as the availability of nearby private schools and the satisfaction with public schools also affect the number of parents who apply for scholarships. However, it is not clear how to adjust for these other factors, and our estimates are based on the distribution of income.

The second element — the share of scholarship recipients who would not have attended public schools — can be informed by lottery-based research. The reason that these "non-switchers" are important is that the Commonwealth's savings rely on a reduction in public school enrollment. If a student uses a scholarship to leave homeschooling, or if the student would have attended a private school without the scholarship, the state does not realize any savings.

The best basis for estimating the number of non-switchers comes from random assignment studies of several private school choice programs. As noted earlier, switcher rates among private school choice programs tend to be quite high — lower-bound and upper-bound weighted average switcher rates are 84 percent and 90 percent.[232]

The estimates below evaluate the fiscal impact on the state and school districts from a scholarship program assuming:

- 10,000 scholarships awarded in the first year (about 1 percent of the state's public school enrollment)
- 90 percent credit rate
- Average scholarship = $4,500
- State provides $40.5 million in tax credits to generate $45 million in donations for scholarships
- Average state cost per student for TCS = $4,050
- 20 percent of students are non-switchers who would have attended private school without a scholarship
- Average foundation budget per student = $12,000[233]
- Target aid in average district with TCS students residing = 70 percent (average state aid per student = $8,400)
- Average short-run variable costs per student = $13,800

As stated previously, a TCS program would have very little impact on the *required* local contribution in cities and towns. However, if large numbers of students left for private schools, municipalities could choose to adjust their spending.

A hold harmless policy will reduce the amount the state saves, but it is difficult to model the exact impact of the hold harmless policy because it depends on the number of students leaving each district. Some districts may be protected from all or part of the reduction in aid, and the actual impact will be between the two extremes in Figure 1.

Figure 1: Fiscal Impact of Model TCS Program

	Hold Harmless	No Hold Harmless
Number of scholarships	10,000	10,000
Donations required to fund scholarships	$45,000,000	$45,000,000
Tax credits disbursed	$40,500,000	$40,500,000
Cost of TCS per student	$4,050	$4,050
Fiscal impact on state		
Number of switchers	8,000	8,000
Avg. Chapter 70 funding per pupil	$12,000	$12,000
State aid reduction per pupil	$8,400	$8,400
State savings from reduced aid payments	$67,200,000	$67,200,000
Hold harmless payments	$67,200,000	$0
Net fiscal impact on state	($40,500,000)	$26,700,000
Net fiscal impact on state per student	($4,050)	$2,670
Fiscal impact on districts		
District short-run AVC PP	$13,800	$13,800
Short-run variable cost savings	$110,400,000	$110,400,000
Reduction in Chapter 70 revenue	$96,000,000	$96,000,000
Hold harmless payments	$67,200,000	$0
Net fiscal impact on districts	$81,600,000	$14,400,000
Net fiscal impact on districts per switcher	$10,200	$1,800

In a world without hold harmless, this program is structured to generate net savings for state taxpayers ($31 million, or $3,120 per student in this particular example). With a hold harmless provision, the state would incur a net cost equal up to the total cost of the TCS program. Any savings the state might incur are offset, to an extent, by the cost of hold harmless.

School districts would experience net fiscal benefits. Although revenue for districts would decline by $12,000 on average for each student leaving, variable cost savings from having fewer students to serve would more than offset this impact. Under hold harmless, districts retain up to $67 million in state aid payments for students leaving them, resulting in $82 million in net fiscal benefits, or about $10,000 per student.

Conclusion

The consensus of high-quality research is that educational choice programs increase student achievement, graduation rates, and college matriculation, and parents of students in such programs report very high levels of satisfaction with their chosen schools. Educational choice also benefits students who remain in the public schools because of increased competition.

The model tax-credit scholarship program proposed in this chapter would expand educational opportunities for tens of thousands of low-income children while remaining revenue neutral or saving money for the state and only minimally impacting school districts. The program would grant tax credits to individual and corporate taxpayers worth 90 percent of their donations to qualified scholarship organizations.

A tax-credit scholarship program would help provide low-income families with opportunities more like those already available to their higher-income peers. It would allow these low-income families to choose the school that best meets the individual needs of their children.

✕ ✕ ✕

Ken Ardon, Ph.D., is a professor of economics at Salem State University, where he has taught since 2004, as well as a member of Pioneer Institute's Center for School Reform Advisory Board. He received a Ph.D. in Economics from the University of California at Santa Barbara in 1999, where he coauthored a book on school spending and student achievement. He taught economics at Pomona College before moving to Massachusetts. From 2000 to 2004, Dr. Ardon worked for the Commonwealth of Massachusetts in the Executive Office of Administration and Finance.

Jason Bedrick is director of policy for EdChoice. Previously, Bedrick served as policy analyst with the Cato Institute's Center for Educational Freedom. He also served as a legislator in the New Hampshire House of Representatives and was an education policy research fellow at the Josiah Bartlett Center for Public Policy. Bedrick received his Master's in Public Policy from the John F. Kennedy School of Government at Harvard University, where he was a fellow at the Taubman Center for State and Local Government.

Martin F. Lueken, Ph.D., is the Fiscal Research and Education Center at EdChoice. He holds a Doctor of Education in Education Policy from the University of Arkansas and a Master's in Economics from the University of Missouri. He studies school finance and the fiscal effects of private school choice programs. He has testified before numerous state legislatures and committees about private school choice bills being introduced. Dr. Lueken's work also includes analysis of teacher pensions, the distribution of retirement benefits, and benefit choice.

Chapter 5:
Cristo Rey Schools: A Model of Twenty-First Century Catholic Education

By Jeff Thielman & William Donovan

Executive Summary

Since the mid-1960s, Catholic high schools in the United States have been separating along different paths based upon their prospects for survival. The pressures of rising labor costs, shifting demographics, and a failing business model have created a distinct alignment consisting of schools serving top and bottom tiers and those catering to a shrinking middle class.

Catholic high schools for upper-income students, with tuitions often exceeding $20,000 per year, enrollments above 1,000 students, and supportive alumni, are holding steady. A middle class of smaller high schools, with enrollments in the low-to-mid hundreds, serving blue-collar families on tuition-sensitive budgets, is being squeezed.

Despite these challenges, schools in the Chicago-based Cristo Rey Network, which serve low-income families in urban areas, are doing what many thought impossible — adding students and opening new schools. While they aren't flush with cash, their nontraditional business model is better than break-even and provides a pathway to college for families who never envisioned it.

"Cristo Rey is a model that many schools admire and look at," said Heather Gossart, director of executive mentoring/coaching and senior consultant with the National Catholic Education Association (NCEA). "It serves those students who would not otherwise be able to access Catholic education. It really does a phenomenal job for what it does."[234]

Cristo Rey schools are returning Catholic education to urban areas. Students receive a college-preparatory education and participate in a work-study program in which they learn employable skills and earn money to help pay for their tuition. Since the first Cristo Rey School was founded in Chicago in 1996, 36 others have opened in 23 states and the District of Columbia, including in Boston and Lawrence.[235]

This chapter will examine how and why Cristo Rey schools work and what parts of their education/business design can be successfully transferred to other Catholic high schools.

Across the country, Catholic high schools have had uneven results attracting new students and bolstering their finances. They've tried tithing by parishioners, hiring professional fundraising firms, diving deep into alumni bases, raising tuitions, and recruiting students from China.[236] Still, the overall numbers are disappointing. During the 10 years prior to the COVID-19 pandemic, more than 100 Catholic secondary schools were closed and just 62 opened. Of those that opened, 23 were Cristo Rey schools.[237, 238]

Background

The roots of the first Cristo Rey school and the Cristo Rey movement stretch back to 1993, when members of the Society of Jesus (the Jesuits) "walked the streets of Chicago's Pilsen neighborhood asking residents how they can best respond to the considerable underserved needs of the Mexican and Latino immigrants pouring into the community," according to Fr. John P. Foley, S.J., founder of the first Cristo Rey high school.[239]

That survey, along with an additional feasibility study, determined that parents wanted a Catholic college preparatory high school. Cristo Rey Jesuit High School opened in August 1996.

According to Fr. Foley, the name "Cristo Rey" (Spanish for "Christ the King") was selected for two reasons: It was appropriate for a high school that would be bilingual, and the image of Christ the King was meaningful for St. Ignatius Loyola, who founded the Jesuit order.[240]

But how would it be financed? Families were unable to afford the tuition of nearly $9,000 per year. So, Fr. Foley and his fellow Jesuits turned to the Chicago business community. They proposed that local employers hire Cristo Rey students to work in clerical capacities, with the fee for their service going directly to the school.

"We went out and knocked on doors and said 'Would you give us a job? Would you hire our students?'" Fr. Foley said. "It started off literally and simple to pay the bills."[241]

But the corporate work-study program took on a more meaningful, transformative role. It became a self-esteem builder as teenagers saw they were earning money to help pay for their own education. They learned office skills in environments in which many had never envisioned themselves working. And they developed interpersonal skills with people outside their peer networks.

Each student worked five eight-hour days per month. Teams of four students shared one 40-hour-per-week, entry-level job. They combined that with 15 days of academic classes per month. The Jesuits designed a school with a longer school day and year to ensure students had enough time for a college preparatory program.

"When you go to any of our schools and say to the kids 'What do you like about our school?' inevitably it's the job," said Fr. Foley. "The kids feel like an adult. They're treated like an adult. They feel like they're part of something and they're taken into account."

Across the Cristo Rey Network, the more than 3,500 corporate partners participating in the work-study program appear to be largely satisfied. The program has an 88 percent annual retention rate and 94 percent of employers said their student employees "meet or exceed" expectations.[242]

A Break With Tradition

This revenue model breaks away from the traditional Catholic school approach that relies on tuition and fundraising. When a Cristo Rey school reaches full enrollment of 400–600 students, 60 percent of revenue is earned through the work-study program, 30 percent through fundraising, and 10 percent from an annual family contribution that averages $1,000.[243]

The work-study program boosts graduation rates: 92 percent of Cristo Rey graduates from the class of 2015 enrolled in college within a year, compared to a national average of 46 percent for low-income students. Cristo Rey students also complete a college education faster than other low-income students. About 44 percent of the Cristo Rey class of 2010 earned a four-year bachelor's degree or two-year associate's degree. That compares with only 12 percent of low-income students nationally.[244]

Cristo Rey schools highlight the high college acceptance and entrance levels of their graduates. But about 39 percent of students who start ninth grade transfer to a different school. Family transience is one reason, but for others the rigor of the program can be too much. Cristo Rey students attend at least the same number of academic hours as public-school students.[245] That expectation, combined with more than 330 work-study hours per year, makes Cristo Rey schools challenging, even though acceptance to college is almost assured when they graduate.

"When students aren't successful in the workplace, they get retraining, one-to-one support, and an opportunity to correct whatever the issue is," said Elizabeth Goettl, president and CEO of the Cristo Rey Network. "But just like in the real world, a student can lose his job and be fired."[246]

But Cristo Rey schools are dedicated to providing a rigorous college preparatory education, and they proudly and exclusively recruit students from families who cannot afford private education. There is a ceiling on family income based on median income in the community. The average annual income for a Cristo Rey family of four is $35,000.

"We don't have those famous problems of parents being

irrationally demanding of the school," said Fr. Foley. "Our kids come from families who are more grateful and humble than you normally see at a private school."

The Cristo Rey student population is overwhelmingly minority, with 97 percent coming from families of color. Latinos and African Americans are the two largest demographic groups.[247] The majority of Latinos are already Catholic, but African Americans usually are not, leading to another surprising statistic: About 45 percent of students throughout the network are not Catholic. Though all students study Catholic theology and religion, Fr. Foley said the schools are "not about proselytizing."

A Cold Reception

"The other Catholic schools got very angry with us when we announced what we were going to do," said Fr. Foley. "They said, 'If you have students come to school, send them to us. We have empty desks.' We said, 'It would never occur to these kids to go to your schools.'"[248]

"We had an awful time selling the idea at the very beginning because of conditions that we ourselves had set up to make peace with the other Catholic schools," Fr. Foley said.

Yet the new school gained national attention. In 2000, venture capitalist B.J. Cassin invested $12 million to create other Cristo Rey schools around the country.

"I told (Fr. Foley) that from the research I had done there was demand for this and we were willing to put a foundation together to replicate the model," Cassin said.[249]

Cassin was sure the Cristo Rey design could be put into a business plan format and fleshed out through a feasibility study to meet demand in urban areas.

Between 2001 and 2009, 23 Cristo Rey schools were started. The first 16 received grants of $400,000 to $600,000 from the Cassin Educational Initiative Foundation. In 2003, the Bill & Melinda Gates Foundation committed $9.9 million, and added $6 million more in 2006.[250] Since that initial surge, the network has grown purposefully and consistently.

Cristo Rey in Massachusetts

Since 2004, two Cristo Rey schools have operated in Massachusetts. Cristo Rey Boston High School, in the Savin Hill neighborhood of Dorchester, is sponsored by the Archdiocese of Boston. Notre Dame Cristo Rey (NDCR) High School in Lawrence is run by the Sisters of Notre Dame de Namur.

In 2015–2016, Cristo Rey Boston students earned more than $2.6 million at 125 businesses and non-profits.[251] Employers pay about $34,800 per year for a team of four students, about $23 per hour, according to John O'Keeffe, director of the work-study program.[252]

In 2016, as in most years before and since, 100 percent of the graduating class was accepted to a four-year college. About 60 percent of the class of 2010 earned an undergraduate degree within six years. That compares with a network average of 44 percent and a national average across all economic strata of 55 percent.[253]

The annual cost to educate a student at Cristo Rey Boston is about $13,000. Tuition ranges from $600 to $3,000 per family, but no family pays full tuition. The average household income of families at Cristo Rey Boston was about $24,800 in 2015.[254]

In Lawrence, the work-study program produced 37 percent or $1.6 million of the school's $4.3 million in revenues for 2016.[255] Donations and other support accounted for 41 percent. For the past eight years NDCR has ranked first among all Cristo Rey schools in workplace performance surveys.[256]

More than 90 percent of NDCR students are Hispanic, with average family income of $35,700. Only 2 percent of students pay the full $3,200 tuition, while more than 60 percent of families pay less than $1,200 per year — though it costs about $12,000 annually to educate a student. Every 2016 graduate was accepted to at least one four-year college, receiving more than $9 million in merit aid — "remarkable" for a graduating class of 68 students, according to Sr. Maryalyce Gilfeather, the school's president.[257]

What Can Be Learned?

Given the success of Massachusetts' Cristo Rey schools, could the Cristo Rey model work for other struggling Catholic high schools?

"Everyone has laudatory remarks for Cristo Rey," said Gossart, "but one size does not fit all in education. At some of our schools that have enrollment challenges, what are ways we can make tuition affordable through financial aid, grants, and creative financing that can get them in the door and help keep them in the door?"[258]

In other words, the Cristo Rey approach probably could not be embraced in total. The work-study approach is not what every Catholic school family wants or needs. Cristo Rey's business practices, however, could be applied elsewhere.

Market Focus Is Critical

Catholic schools in the Archdiocese of Boston, especially those focused on the middle class, need to be very targeted in terms of whom they serve. Carrie Wagner, former vice principal of academics at Cristo Rey Boston, said that fierce school competition in Boston, including charter schools and alternative programs offered by public schools, has put pressure on middle class Catholic high schools.

"The choice makes the middle ground difficult because you have to really be sure of who you serve and what you're offering to that population," she said. "You have to be a pretty targeted program in order to make the financial sacrifice worth it."[259]

The Cristo Rey network will not open in a new city until the employer base is proven, a partner is found, and a feasibility study is completed—such as the 2002 study that determined there was a "critical need" for Cristo Rey schools in Boston and Lawrence.

Cristo Rey schools further define the families they serve through an income formula. To qualify for admission, a student's adjusted family income must fall below 75 percent of the local or national median income, whichever is higher, according to Cristo Rey Network policy. Cities with a high cost of living, such as San Francisco or Boston, have higher income limits.

"The adjustment to family income is run through a third-party income verification service," said Seanna Mullen Sumrak, advancement officer for the Cristo Rey Network in Chicago. "The formula allows for such things as high medical or educational debt or families supporting other adults in the home. Incomes can vary widely depending on a family's specific situation."[260]

Since all the schools in the Cristo Rey Network operate under the same business model, the collective experience is a valuable resource to administrators and faculty members. Leaders and teachers at other Catholic schools attend workshops and forums for professional development, but teachers and staff at Cristo Rey schools act as their own support group, further sharpening their market focus.

"We can do strategic thinking with more than just our school," Sr. Gilfeather. "We meet with other schools struggling with the same things."[261]

Cristo Rey Schools Think Creatively

"With the birth of the Cristo Rey network, I really believe it was the creative way of getting Catholic schools back in the inner cities working with the poor, where we need to be," said Sr. Gilfeather. "I believe that's really the calling of the Church."

The corporate work-study program was proposed simply as a way to pay the bills but has become the financial foundation. Moreover, the Cristo Rey management model was developed to support schools that also function as job-placement agencies.

The school president is the primary representative to external audiences and is responsible for finances. The principal oversees academic and student life and is coequal to the director of work-study. The development director and chief financial officer are also coequals. The president appoints and supervises all four roles.

Cristo Rey Boston is located near public transportation, providing easy access to students' employers. Lawrence is much different. The smaller number of companies there makes the work-study program more difficult to operate.

"We went into this with our eyes wide open, knowing that getting jobs was going to be a struggle and we were going to have to go much further than most Cristo Rey schools needed to go to find jobs," said Sr. Gilfeather.

Each morning, students board 10 vans and two cars and travel as much as 30 miles in all directions to their 75 companies.

Cristo Rey judges applicants not only by their academic history, but by the likelihood of employability. If they seem suitable, they participate in a mandatory two-week summer training program, taking classes on hard and soft office skills, making good impressions, and demonstrating a proper attitude.

"In the interview we make sure they understand what kind of jobs they're getting into," said Julia White, corporate work-study coordinator at NDCR.

Addressing Students' Challenges

Cristo Rey schools can create academic programs to meet their students' needs. Teachers and academic leaders know the socio-economic backgrounds and family structures of their families. And the Cristo Rey Network works with schools to devise academic programs.

"They have also done a great deal in helping us understand second language learners," said Sr. Gilfeather, "as well as single-parent family learners where the woman is the one who is predominantly the caretaker."

To ramp up learning, NDCR has its Academic Support and Assistance Program (ASAP), in which students report to school five days each week during the first marking period. On the day when they would normally work, they receive instruction in math skills, reading, grammar and usage, study skills, and computer use.

Notre Dame Cristo Rey has also created the Center for Academic Support and Assistance (CASA), which provides students with the opportunity to strengthen basic skills in mathematics, vocabulary, English grammar and usage, reading, and writing.

Many students who attend Cristo Rey schools work after-school jobs or assist in caretaking at home. For those students, NDCR created the Early Bird Academic Recovery Program, which begins at 6:33 a.m.

Lastly, NDCR created a program that requires all ninth graders to attend two evenings of study skills during the week prior to mid-terms and final exams. "All of our teachers know they need to bring our students up at least two grade levels each year in order for the students to be prepared for college," said Sr. Gilfeather.

Cristo Rey Boston initiated a proficiency program designed to get ninth graders ready for the rigors of a college preparatory program. Each August, every entering ninth grader takes a proficiency test. While a small number pass, most do not and are assigned a volunteer tutor. They take the exam each month until they pass.[262]

In addition to the proficiency program, every ninth grader at Cristo Rey Boston takes double-block classes of math and English. Each academic department — math, English, science, foreign language (Spanish), history — offers an Advanced Placement (AP) course during senior year, and every senior is required to take at least one AP course.

Each spring, most Cristo Rey schools tout the achievement of all their graduates being accepted into at least one four-year school. But Wagner said simply being accepted isn't acceptable.

"Getting 100 percent accepted does not mean we've done our job in getting them prepared for college," Wagner said. "What helps us understand if we are doing our job is whether they are able to earn their degree and graduate from college."[263]

Yet the ability to earn a degree sometimes isn't enough for low-income students. Cristo Rey schools have found that many students will complete a year or two of college before the financial burden becomes overwhelming. During the 2016–2017 school year, Cristo Rey Boston's college counselor advised families to consider other financial options if they needed to take out more than $7,000 per year in loans.[264]

"The name of the school is not the most important thing," said Wagner. "It's the fit of the school that is. We work very hard with students to get them the best possible financial package that we can."

Faculty and Staff Are on a Mission

Elena Zongrone, director of development at Cristo Rey Boston, thinks the difference between her school and other Catholic schools is the mission. When she speaks with potential donors she talks about "changing the trajectory" of the lives of low-income students through a Cristo Rey education. Elite Catholic high schools have large parent populations who can donate to the school. Cristo Rey does not.

"Our parents are more than happy to help in any way they can, but in actual donation of dollars that's not an option for them," she said. "We have to look at people who believe in the mission, who believe in Catholic education, and who believe in taking kids and offering them a better opportunity than maybe has been presented to the parents."[265]

Rebecca Twitchell, marketing director and interim development director at NDCR, acknowledges that her school does not have the alumni base or parent donors of other Catholic high schools. But the work motivates her colleagues.

"Our story is very clear and our mission is very clear," she said. "The Sisters of Notre Dame de Namur are about serving the poor through education."[266]

Teachers at Cristo Rey Boston earn $45,000 to $65,000 per year, according to Wagner. The school often loses people who move on to higher-paying jobs. She said it is difficult to diversify the staff and hire more people of color, because the Boston Public Schools recruit aggressively, and Cristo Rey can't match the starting salaries.

"People don't come here to make money," Wagner said. "If that's a top priority then people are looking elsewhere. People work here because they believe in the work we're doing."

Sometimes people previously employed in higher-paying

sectors join the school because they're looking for a meaningful change. John O'Keeffe, director of the work-study program at Cristo Rey Boston, previously worked for a Boston investment firm, selling mutual funds. He saw an advertisement for his position and went for it as "an opportunity to give something back."

All that is not to say there isn't turnover at Cristo Rey Schools. O'Keeffe has been on the job for a year at Cristo Rey Boston, as has Zongrone as director of development. In Lawrence, Rebecca Twitchell is the marketing director at NDCR, but currently the interim development director as well. Cristo Rey Boston began the 2017–2018 school year with its third new president in three years, and a new principal. Finding leaders of Catholic schools is always a challenge, but Cristo Rey schools in particular depend on mission-driven people willing to work long hours and serve low-income students.

Conclusion

Cristo Rey schools were formed for families who wanted a Catholic education for their children but couldn't afford the tuition. Since 1996, Cristo Rey schools have separated themselves from most other Catholic schools by staying true to those families.

Defenders of middle- and upper-income Catholic schools say they educate students who will one day be in positions to help others such as the poor. Sr. Gilfeather agrees but makes a further point about Cristo Rey schools.

"I have never seen any metric that said how many graduated (from those schools) and this is all the good they're doing for the poor," she said. "I can give you the metric for how many poor kids I have and how many poor kids get to college and through college. The (return on investment) here is a miracle. You see what you're doing."

In her book *Putting Education to Work: How Cristo Rey High Schools Are Transforming Urban Education*, journalist Megan Sweas states that one of the reasons Catholic schools did not broaden their curriculum was the belief, "intrinsic to the Catholic faith," that "all deserve and are capable of receiving a classical education that advances their spiritual understanding."

Sweas cites the study "Catholic Schools and the Common Good," by Anthony Bryk, Valerie Lee, and Peter Holland, who wrote that "such intellectual development was deemed necessary in order to grasp fully the established understandings about person, society, and God."[267]

While that mission remains essential, it is the financial model that makes it possible in Cristo Rey schools. The 2002 feasibility study described the conditions in which a school would be started:

"A Cristo Rey school must demonstrate an ability to reach students not currently served by Catholic high schools and to increase the total number of students and families receiving a Catholic education. Furthermore, the fuel that makes a Cristo Rey school go is revenue from the work-study program, which represents a business expense, not a charitable contribution, for a corporation. The experience in fundraising apart from the work-study in (other Cristo Rey cities) is that Cristo Rey attracts new donors who previously have not given to Catholic education."[268]

Recommendations: Lessons for Other Catholic Schools
Define your market

Cristo Rey schools are one organization with two clearly defined markets: students and employers. Sharp understanding of their students helps Cristo Rey administrators tailor their programs to their students' needs and tell a compelling story to donors and corporate work-study program partners. They also match their schools to their communities. Cristo Rey Boston, for example, reaches out to more public and charter middle schools since many Catholic middle schools have closed.

Struggling Catholic schools might stabilize their enrollment declines by developing a target student population, educating students with similar challenges and motivations.

Establish your brand

It is not sacrilegious for a Catholic school to consider what it does in commercial terms. Cristo Rey schools are known as the Catholic schools that serve disadvantaged students. Catholic is who they are; educating the less advantaged is what they do. There is a Cristo Rey national logo and "mission effectiveness standards" that all schools follow.

But the number one reason listed for parents sending their children to Catholic secondary schools is academic excellence. As Gossart said: "Our product has to be competitive in the marketplace for us to survive."

Be rigorous but find ways to respond to students who struggle

Both Cristo Rey Boston and Notre Dame Cristo Rey High School, along with other schools in the Cristo Rey Network, have designed their curricula to accommodate the overwhelming number of students who come to school below grade level. Remarkably, Cristo Rey schools have succeeded in getting students into college. Rather than searching for students overseas, could traditional Catholic schools learn something from Cristo Rey and become places not just for good students, but for those who struggle? Such an approach could revolutionize their academic programs and make them attractive to a whole new market.

Jeff Thielman is the President and CEO of the International Institute of New England (IINE), which provides resettlement, education, career pathways, and legal services to 2,500 refugees and immigrants each year in Massachusetts and New Hampshire. Prior to joining IINE, Thielman cofounded the national Cristo Rey Network, oversaw start-up of the first 24 Cristo Rey schools, and served as President of Cristo Rey Boston High School. He has been a trial attorney, worked in financial services, and spent three years as a Jesuit International Volunteer in Tacna, Peru. Thielman is the coauthor of *Volunteer: With the Poor in Peru*, and holds undergraduate and law degrees from Boston College.

William Donovan is a former staff writer with the *Providence Journal* in Rhode Island, where he wrote about business and government. He has taught business journalism in the graduate programs at Boston University and Northeastern University. He received his undergraduate degree from Boston College and his Master's in Journalism from American University in Washington, D.C.

Chapter 6:
Modeling Urban Scholarship Vouchers in the Commonwealth

By Ken Ardon, Ph.D. & Cara Stillings Candal, Ed.D.

Introduction

The United States is one of the few industrialized nations in which parents do not have a fundamental right to choose the publicly funded schools their children attend.[269] The system of school funding in the U.S. relies heavily on revenue generated at the local level. This means that localities with higher home values can generate tax revenue with comparatively less effort than communities where homes are not as valuable; as a result, wealthier communities often have better resourced schools. While there is no clear relationship between school funding and student outcomes, schools in wealthier districts across the country tend to outperform their counterparts in less privileged communities.[270]

When they have the ability to do so, many parents choose schools by moving from one community to another or sending their children to a private school. When families cannot afford to do either of these things, they are left with more limited educational opportunities.

Some school choice advocates view the ability to choose a school as a fundamental right and a social justice issue. They believe it unfair that families who cannot afford to live in wealthy communities should be denied the ability to send their child to a school that meets his or her distinct needs. They also posit that increased choice will provide incentives for all schools to become better. Various opponents of school choice fear that allowing parents to opt out of the public system will take money away from districts, leaving some to be "dumping grounds" for the students who are most "difficult" to educate.[271]

Public magnet schools, charter schools, and other public school choice programs have increased options for many families. Homeschooling is another option, but can be costly when a parent who might otherwise generate income stays home to educate their children.

Some states have begun to make it easier for families to send their children to private schools through vouchers, education savings accounts (ESAs), and scholarship tax credit programs.[272]

Vouchers provide public funds (often state and local) to parents to help pay tuition at private schools. ESAs do the same (usually using state funds only) but allow funds to be used for a variety of educational expenses, including but not limited to private school tuition. Scholarship tax credits work indirectly by providing a tax credit to a third party that donates money to fund a scholarship that is provided to parents.

Though many Massachusetts communities provide intra-district choice, magnet schools, and charter schools, the state Constitution has traditionally made it impossible to enact a program of private school choice. In 2020, the U.S. Supreme Court, in *Espinoza v. Montana Department of Revenue*, invalidated most state constitutional barriers to providing public funding for private schools — the so-called Blaine Amendments. Massachusetts's Blaine Amendment, however, is particularly strong, and it is not yet clear whether *Espinoza* will apply here.

Nonetheless, as private school choice programs blossom around the country, it is increasingly pertinent to ask how a system of private school choice could provide more options for Massachusetts parents.

Private School Choice in the U.S.

According to the American Federation for Children, the number and variety of private school choice programs across the country has grown rapidly in recent years. The programs began approximately 25 years ago when the Milwaukee Parental Choice Program offered a means-tested voucher for low-income children who want to attend private school.

During the 1990s, private school choice grew slowly. By 2000, fewer than 30,000 students had access to private school choice programs in four states. Since that time, growth has accelerated as governors signed into law new programs or expanded existing programs. By 2019, 26 states, Puerto Rico, and Washington, D.C. had private school choice programs, almost all of which are designed to provide more choice to low-income students and students with special educational needs.[273]

School Choice in Massachusetts

Massachusetts offers residents several public school choice programs, including intra-district choice programs, interdistrict (open enrollment) choice programs, vocational-technical school options, and charter public schools. Additionally, roughly 3,000 students participate in Metropolitan Council for Educational Opportunity (METCO), the state's voluntary integration program, which allows students in Boston and Springfield to attend school in other participating (mainly suburban) communities.[274] At this time, Massachusetts has no private school choice programs to support the more than 100,000 students enrolled in private schools across the Commonwealth.[275]

Median household income in Massachusetts is roughly $60,000, and for households with children it is approximately $85,000.[276] Statewide, roughly 30 percent of households have income below 200 percent of the federal poverty guidelines, and in Boston the median income for households with children is only $40,000.[277] While there are many low-cost religious private schools in Massachusetts, most low-income families cannot afford to pay full tuition.

The COVID-19 pandemic of 2020 exacerbated this issue: Families who are dissatisfied with district approaches to remote and hybrid learning seek private school alternatives. Families who find open spots in those schools have to be able to afford the cost of tuition. Most low-income families are left with only their district alternative.[278]

A 2012 poll conducted for Pioneer Institute by DAPA Research identified that over two-thirds of 500 likely voters believe that "less affluent families should have access to options other than their local public school."[279] Likewise, two-thirds of respondents expressed support for charter schools and for "allowing the families of mostly poor and minority children in failing schools to use part of the money that would have been spent educating their child to send their child to any public, private, or parochial school willing to accept him or her."

These data are supported by more recent national polls, which show increasing support for all types of school choice. A 2019 American Federation for Children poll put support for school choice nationally at 67 percent.[280]

Among the public school choice options for Massachusetts families, vocational education (voc-tech) is becoming increasingly popular. In 2019, roughly 60,000 Massachusetts students were enrolled in voc-tech schools in the Commonwealth.[281] Demand for voc-tech schools is high; many have long waiting lists and requirements for admission.[282]

By law, parents in Massachusetts have the right to enroll their children in a school district other than that in which they live. However, their ability to exercise that right is dependent upon several factors, including a receiving district's ability and willingness to accommodate additional students.

According to the Massachusetts Department of Elementary and Secondary Education (DESE), the number of pupils taking advantage of interdistrict choice has risen dramatically over time; from 920 pupils in 116 sending districts in 1992, to

14,734 pupils from 301 sending districts in 2015.[283] By law, only 2 percent of public school students can use the interdistrict choice program, and the program does not provide transportation.[284]

There is also unmet demand for the METCO program, started in the 1960s to "reduce the racial isolation of suburban school districts and to reduce segregation in city schools." METCO sends students from Boston and Springfield to school districts across the state that agree to receive them. In the 2018–2019 school year, about 33 receiving districts voluntarily participated in the METCO program, serving 3,000 enrolled students.[285] These students represent only a small portion of those who seek access to the program.

On average, participating students "outperform their peers in the schools they left behind and, frequently, the state average."[286] METCO students also graduate high school in fewer years and at greater rates than their peers in sending districts and are more likely to complete college.[287] The vast majority of METCO students are African American (73 percent) and the vast majority of receiving districts are predominantly white.[288] METCO supporters suggest that there are great benefits, cognitive and otherwise, for all students who attend school in a racially mixed environment.[289]

Demand for charter schools in the Commonwealth is unmatched by any other existing school choice option. Much of the demand, especially among African American and Hispanic families of low-income backgrounds, can be attributed to the reputation charter schools have earned for outperforming traditional public schools not only in urban centers but across the state;[290] independent studies have confirmed that Massachusetts charter schools are among some of the highest performing public schools nationwide.[291]

According to DESE, in the 2019–20 school year, more than 37,400 students were enrolled in charter schools statewide, comprising 3.9 percent of the public school student population. In the same year, almost 28,000 students were on charter school waitlists.[292] As with other school choice options, those who take advantage of charter schools tend to reside in lower-performing districts and are from low-income families that are unable to afford private school tuition. For instance, 30 percent of students enrolled in charter schools in Massachusetts are African American and 35 percent are Hispanic, compared to approximately 9 and 21 percent statewide, respectively.[293] Students in Massachusetts charter schools are also overwhelmingly low-income.[294]

When combined, the waiting lists for all public-school choice options in Massachusetts comprise tens of thousands of students. Given such unmet demand, why doesn't the Commonwealth provide more school choice? What are the consequences of failing to provide alternative educational options for students and families?

Rationale for School Choice

For some, the most important rationale for school choice is that it greatly enhances a parent's right to direct the education and rearing of his or her children. Studies show that when parents can choose schools, involvement and satisfaction increase.[295]

Studies have shown that where choice exists, student outcomes are better. Of course, if only motivated families take advantage of school choice, a poorly designed study could overestimate the impact of the choice program, because the students likely would have performed well even without the program. The best way to correct for this potential problem is to use data from oversubscribed programs where a random lottery determines which applicants receive scholarships.

A large number of the high-quality studies based on random assignment have shown that many different types of school choice programs have positive effects on student achievement.[296, 297]

When combined with research suggesting that choice programs (including charter schools) promote civic values such as tolerance, volunteerism, and political knowledge, the argument for leveraging choice to enhance both cognitive and non-cognitive student outcomes is even more compelling. Some voucher programs slightly *reduce* racial segregation, as minority students move from public schools that are racially homogenous to private schools that serve more heterogeneous student populations.[298]

Despite claims that school choice programs damage public school systems by diverting needed funding and the most motivated pupils to private schools, researchers generally find the opposite to be true.

Stanford University Professor Caroline Hoxby, for example, found that competition, whether from vouchers, charters, or other public schools, improved the performance of public schools.[299] The magnitude of the impact was large, indicating that increased competition would help the average student in public schools even if the private schools skimmed off only the highest performing students. Similarly, Gray et al. found that the CEO Horizon Scholarship in San Antonio had a small but significant positive spillover effect on the traditional public schools.[300]

In Massachusetts, those who are demanding school choice are those most likely to be trapped in failing schools. Although in the past 25 years many Massachusetts school districts have made dramatic achievement gains, 301 struggling schools still serve predominantly poor and minority students, the same students who are on long waitlists. The lack of supply presents a social justice issue.

There is also evidence that not all the choices available even to these students are similar or equal to those available to wealthier families. For example, even where charter public schools provide an alternative to the traditional district schools, it is unclear that they provide the innovative educational options that many families seek.

This is complicated by a clause in the 2010 *Act Relative to the Achievement Gap* that allows only "proven providers" to establish new charter schools in low-performing districts.[302] Many of these providers favor similar pedagogical approaches, meaning the diverse approaches to schooling in the private sector are largely unavailable to families who cannot afford private school tuition.

Some argue that this lack of choice presents an economic problem, since students trapped in failing schools will be less prepared for the workforce. Fewer opportunities for vocational-technical education, for example, can create a drag on the economy. Researchers note long waitlists for vocational schools in communities with high unemployment.[303]

Unfortunately, Massachusetts is one of many states that has erected legal barriers to the kinds of private school choice that have proven beneficial to students elsewhere.

Legal Barriers to Private School Choice in Massachusetts

In the 2002 *Zelman v. Harris-Simmons* decision, the Supreme Court of the United States ruled that a state "does not violate the Establishment Clause by providing funding to a religiously affiliated school," as long as the program meets certain legal criteria, such as "being neutral with respect to religion and providing assistance to a broad range of citizens."[304]

Although this ruling made way for voucher programs in some states, Massachusetts remains one of many states that have failed to repeal the laws and amendments, rooted in anti-Catholic sentiment and bigotry, that are described in Chapter 2. While many states will be now be forced to repeal Blaine Amendments in the wake of the Supreme Court's decision in the aforementioned *Espinoza* case, the Commonwealth's very strong Anti-Aid Amendment is likely to remain, at least for the near future.

The hurdle that Massachusetts citizens who favor private school choice would have to clear is a high one, despite the benefits that an enhanced system of school choice could bring in the form of productive competition for public schools and the potential for better student outcomes overall.

Nonetheless, if demand for school choice continues to increase at the current rate, and if school voucher and voucher-like programs continue to be levers that other states successfully pull for education reform, a future challenge to the state's Anti-Aid Amendment could succeed.

Understanding what a voucher program might look like in Massachusetts and understanding its potential impacts are important steps in supporting any future effort to repeal the Know-Nothing Amendment.

A Scholarship Voucher Program for Massachusetts

State-funded vouchers would significantly expand school choice. A voucher program involves many important details that affect the program's benefits and costs, and perhaps the most important is the answer to one critical question: Who is eligible?

In addition to student or family characteristics, voucher programs sometimes restrict eligibility based on the student's local district — e.g., they may be only for students in underperforming districts.

Finally, the program could be restricted only to students previously enrolled in public schools, or it could also be open to families whose children already attend a private school. While there are many possibilities open to policy makers, the analysis below will examine how a voucher program for low-income families in urban areas would affect state and local finances.

In addition to determining eligibility, program designers must also decide on the value of the voucher. Vouchers can vary by the student's age — e.g., smaller for elementary schools and larger for high schools, as is the case for the D.C. Scholarship Opportunity Program — or by family income to provide larger vouchers to lower-income families. Research published by Pioneer Institute in 2014 found that the median private school tuition in low-income cities was about $6,000 in grades K–8 and about $8,600 in grades 9–12.[305]

If the voucher is too small, many families will not be able to afford private school and the program will not expand school choice. On the other hand, if the voucher is larger the program could become more expensive, meaning that fewer families and children might benefit.

The connection between the size of the voucher and the cost of the program is not straightforward — the state may reduce aid to local districts when students leave, which offsets the cost of the vouchers. That can result in little or no impact on net cost to the state, although it reduces funds available to local districts. In some cases, even generous vouchers can reduce total spending on education. However, any savings from vouchers are offset if vouchers are awarded to families who would have sent their children to private school even without the voucher.

Despite having some of the best public schools in the country, more students attend private schools in Massachusetts than in other states. However, a large majority of private school students come from upper- or middle-income families.[306] A means-tested voucher program in Massachusetts could greatly expand educational choice to families that cannot afford private school today.

There are many low-income students in Massachusetts public schools; almost 40 percent of students live with families eligible for free or reduced-price lunch. If the Commonwealth offered a significant voucher to these families, there would undoubtedly be more applicants than slots available.

Based on the estimates of the cost of private school and the size of vouchers in other states, vouchers of $6,000 to K–8 students and $8,000 to high school students might be appropriate. If these were offered to families with income below 200 percent of the federal poverty guidelines, roughly 350,000 students would be eligible.

The program rules could determine whether vouchers were available to all public school students, only those in targeted urban areas, or perhaps those in low-performing districts. Even if the program were available statewide, the majority of applicants would most likely come from urban areas.

A voucher program for 10,000 urban participants might draw enrollees from the districts as illustrated in Figure 1.

It would represent just 3.7 percent of enrollment in these cities and involve only 4.2 percent of their low-income students. Vouchers for 10,000 students would require about $67 million in state funds annually.[307] However, estimates from existing programs demonstrate that voucher programs are likely to reduce total spending.[308]

Enrollment declines in some public districts that would result from a voucher program could be handled by the state's Chapter 70 formula, but would lead to erratic and inequitable outcomes.[309] A simpler system would be to reduce state aid to districts by the amount of the voucher, exactly offsetting reduced state aid. While local districts would see a reduction in state aid, vouchers are much lower than average per-pupil spending, meaning districts would still be left with more funds to spend on their remaining students.

Figure 1: Example of Distribution of Vouchers

City	Voucher Recipients	Percent of Enrollment
Boston	2,383	3.7%
Brockton	685	3.9%
Cambridge	164	2.4%
Chelsea	288	4.2%
Everett	279	3.7%
Fall River	442	3.9%
Lawrence	639	4.2%
Lowell	580	3.8%
Lynn	648	4.0%
Malden	223	3.0%
Medford	89	1.8%
New Bedford	509	3.9%
Peabody	108	1.8%
Quincy	243	2.6%
Salem	139	3.0%
Somerville	191	3.5%
Springfield	1,257	4.3%
Waltham	117	2.2%
Worcester	1,016	3.7%
Total	**10,000**	**3.7%**

Figure 2: Potential Changes in State Aid and Spending Per Pupil

City	FY16 Required Spending Per Pupil	Reduction in State Aid	Spending Per Pupil After Vouchers	Increase in Spending Per Pupil
Boston	$13,547	$15,966,100	$13,811	$264
Brockton	$11,839	$4,589,500	$12,046	$207
Cambridge	$11,547	$1,098,800	$11,665	$118
Chelsea	$12,178	$1,929,600	$12,416	$238
Everett	$11,972	$1,869,300	$12,176	$204
Fall River	$11,572	$2,961,400	$11,770	$198
Lawrence	$12,257	$4,281,300	$12,501	$244
Lowell	$11,668	$3,886,000	$11,864	$196
Lynn	$11,970	$4,341,600	$12,192	$222
Malden	$11,367	$1,494,100	$11,512	$145
Medford	$11,575	$596,300	$11,665	$90
New Bedford	$11,316	$3,410,300	$11,501	$185
Peabody	$10,807	$723,600	$10,883	$76
Quincy	$11,959	$1,628,100	$12,100	$141
Salem	$11,359	$931,300	$11,502	$143
Somerville	$13,681	$1,279,700	$13,937	$256
Springfield	$11,929	$8,421,900	$12,166	$237
Waltham	$11,744	$783,900	$11,858	$114
Worcester	$12,002	$6,807,200	$12,205	$204
Average	**$12,246**	**$67,000,000**	**$12,456**	**$210**

Figure 2 illustrates the impact on state aid and per-pupil spending of the voucher program described above. Per-student spending in the affected districts would rise by an average of $210. This does not necessarily mean remaining students would have more resources, depending, for example, upon how many children with more expensive special education needs were to use vouchers.

However, the small changes in Figure 2 demonstrate that the overall impact on per-student funding is small. The more important effect is that increased competition could have significant benefits for the vast majority of students who would not use vouchers—the 260,000 eligible students remaining in the public schools.

Conclusion and Recommendations

Many Massachusetts families have little choice about where their children attend school. More than 50,000 mostly urban students are on waiting lists for vocational schools, charter schools, and the METCO program, and an untold number of other families would be interested in private school choice. States that have implemented private school choice in the past two decades have almost always chosen to expand their initial programs.

A voucher program such as the one described in this chapter would allow 10,000 students to attend private school. The program could target low-income students, students with special needs, and students in failing districts.

There is abundant evidence that private school choice increases parents' satisfaction, and that students using vouchers or ESAs receive an education that on average is at least as good as, if not better than, that provided in the public schools. These outcomes are particularly likely because the families least satisfied with their local schools would be most likely to use vouchers. And research from other states suggests that traditional public schools thrive when faced with additional competition.

To expand school choice, particularly for low-income and minority students and families, we recommend that the Legislature:

- Repeal the 1855 and 1917 Know-Nothing Amendments that prevent the Commonwealth from moving forward with vouchers and expanded urban school choice.
- Create a voucher program based on the best practices and most successful voucher and ESA programs in other states.

- Collect adequate data to monitor and evaluate the program's effects on participants and on public school districts.

Vouchers would offer parents additional choice, supplement existing charter and vocational school options, and have no effect on families that are satisfied with their local public schools. The impact on enrollment in any specific district would be small, and could be further limited by program design. The financial impact, as shown in the figures above, is minimal.

Vouchers have the potential to increase family satisfaction, reduce racial isolation, and strengthen educational outcomes for both the recipients and the children remaining in public schools—at little or no net cost to taxpayers. More fundamentally, they could provide low-income families with the choices that other families already possess. It is time for the Commonwealth to consider expanding private school choice.

✣ ✣ ✣

Ken Ardon, Ph.D., is a professor of economics at Salem State University, where he has taught since 2004, as well as a member of Pioneer Institute's Center for School Reform Advisory Board. He received a Ph.D. in Economics from the University of California at Santa Barbara in 1999, where he coauthored a book on school spending and student achievement. He taught economics at Pomona College before moving to Massachusetts. From 2000 to 2004, Dr. Ardon worked for the Commonwealth of Massachusetts in the Executive Office of Administration and Finance.

Cara Stillings Candal, Ed.D., has spent the last 10 years working in education policy as a Senior Fellow with both Pioneer Institute and the Center for Education Reform. She was also a founding team member of the National Academy of Advanced Teacher Education (NAATE) and a research assistant professor at Boston University in the Department of Educational Leadership and Development. Candal has authored/edited more than 25 papers and three books on education policy. She earned a Bachelor of Arts in English Literature from Indiana University, a Master of Arts in Social Science from the University of Chicago, and a Doctor of Education from Boston University. Candal is the author most recently of Pioneer Institute's book, *The Fight for the Best Charter Public Schools in the Nation*.

Chapter 7:
The Healing Hand: Modeling Catholic Medical Vocational-Technical Schooling

By Alison Fraser & Bill Donovan

Executive Summary

Historically, Catholic college preparatory and career vocational-technical schools have had contrasting approaches to secondary school education. Catholic schools have provided classical liberal arts education, including religious instruction, with emphasis on the spiritual and intellectual potential of every student and an eye towards higher education. Voc-tech programs have been for kids who weren't "college material," weren't plunging into Shakespeare or the arts, and who intended to find a career in the trades.

In the Archdiocese of Boston today, many Catholic high schools are struggling with enrollment declines. Meanwhile, public career vocational technical education (CVTE) schools in Massachusetts are thriving, some with long waiting lists.

The ironic outcome is that Catholic school leaders are starting to see voc-tech education as a way to stop their enrollment slide—although not by opening multi-discipline voc-tech schools or adding a costly robotics or metal fabrication course.

Rather, they are considering a medical arts program, where the barriers to entry are lower and opportunities are abundant.

But questions persist: Is it affordable? Is it manageable? Is it Catholic?

Catholic schools are successful runways for college-bound students. According to the Archdiocese of Boston, Catholic high school students had an average SAT score of 1605 in 2016, higher than Massachusetts (1552) and national (1484) averages. Among archdiocese Advanced Placement (AP) students, 75 percent scored a 3 or higher (which normally makes the student eligible for college credit) on at least one exam, better than state (71 percent) and national (60 percent) averages. About 97 percent of Archdiocese students graduate, and 96 percent of graduates go to college.

Yet business is slumping at many of the Archdiocese's high schools. Enrollment fell 11 percent from 2002 to 2017. Many former Catholic school families are moving to the suburbs and sending their children to public high schools. Catholic school payrolls have risen as nuns and priests have been replaced by lay teachers. And the clergy abuse scandal meant the end of subsidies. That has left the schools — ineligible for public funding — to rely on tuitions, fundraising, and grants.

Meanwhile, vocational-technical education in Massachusetts has surged, in part because a 1993 reform measure required voc-tech students to pass the same Massachusetts Comprehensive Assessment System (MCAS) tests as college prep students. Voc-tech dropout rates are significantly lower than traditional high schools,[310] and students often have a job waiting upon graduation. Waiting lists have swelled into the thousands.

Catholic education leaders have noticed the rise in CVTE popularity and understand the economic opportunities that await graduates, but they worry about blurring their reputation for college preparation. Nationwide, Catholic school seniors score an average of 20 and 26 points higher in math and reading than their public school counterparts on the National Assessment of Educational Progress (NAEP), and an average 45, 43, and 53 points higher on math, reading, and writing SAT assessments, respectively.[311]

"That has always been the brand that has identified us, so there has been a little bit of pause when you think about the public perception if we were to introduce vocational education into a Catholic high school," says Heather Gossart, senior consultant with the National Catholic Education Association.[312]

The Archdiocese of Boston recently commissioned a study to explore voc-tech education. Then-superintendent Kathy Mears thought it was a good idea.

"There's a New England bias looking down on vocational education," she said. "But the Catholic Church believes in the dignity of work and that all work is good. There is no shame in not having a degree from Harvard."[313]

This chapter explores the merits of and financial and facilities requirements of medical voc-tech education for Catholic high schools. Health services include nurse aide training, dental assisting, medical laboratory assisting, and electrocardiogram (EKG) technician training.

There is only one traditional career voc-tech education Catholic high school in the U.S.—Mercy Career & Technical High School in Philadelphia. There had been others, including Don Bosco Technical High School in Boston, which closed in 1998. Voc-tech instruction in Catholic schools today means programs in computer science or biotechnology at college prep schools. Yet that may be about to change.

Background

Since seeing enrollment peak in the early 1960s, when more than 5.2 million students attended nearly 13,000 Catholic schools nationwide, Catholic school enrollments have declined and many schools have closed.

But as Archdiocese of Boston schools have struggled, the number of students in voc-tech education has been climbing. In 2011, there were 44,175 students in Chapter 74-approved programs in regional CVTE schools, district vocational, or traditional public high schools.[314] By 2018, there were 48,750, a 10.4 percent increase over 2011.

David Ferreira, executive director of the Massachusetts Association of Vocational Administrators (MAVA), said the increase was probably limited by lack of sufficient seats to meet demand.[315]

Politicians and business leaders view voc-tech education as a way to raise employment and address a skilled labor shortage. In January 2016, Governor Charlie Baker announced $83.5 million in funding for career vocational education over five years,[316] including $9.3 million in workforce skills equipment grants to 35 high schools, community colleges, and vocational training providers.[317] The state also provided another $11.8 million in taxpayer revenue in March 2017 for 32 vocational schools, community colleges, and traditional public high schools to purchase equipment and expand training.[318]

A coalition of business groups, community organizations, and vocational high school administrators has formed the Alliance for Vocational Technical Education to promote CVTE. They raised $60,000 to fund a study at Northeastern University about public perceptions of voc-tech education.[319] A survey of more than 350 Massachusetts employers found some 90 percent saw a need to increase the number of voc-tech graduates and provide voc-tech schools with more modern equipment.[320]

The Commonwealth's CVTE health services cluster includes health, dental, and medical assisting. Students typically prepare for the American Red Cross Certified Nursing Assistant Exam, the National Health Career Association National Certification Exam for EKG Technicians, and the American Heart Association First Aid Certification.

In Massachusetts, 25 of 26 regional voc-tech schools offer courses in the health assisting cluster.[321] Enrollment in health services rose nearly 17 percent from 2011 to 2017, according to the Massachusetts Department of Elementary and Secondary Education (DESE).

According to the latest research from the Massachusetts Executive Office of Workforce and Labor Development, there is a growing need for health and allied health professionals throughout the Commonwealth. Teaching certificate courses in Catholic high schools is a way to ensure both immediate career entry for graduates or a solid background for post-secondary study in the medical arts and sciences.

Students who complete a four-year health assisting program are prepared for entry-level positions leading to careers as an EMT, occupational therapist, or registered nurse. From 2014 to 2024, demand in Massachusetts for home health aides is expected to rise more than 37 percent; for medical assistants, 15 percent; and for physical therapists more than 25 percent.[322]

The High Price of Voc-Tech

Tempting as those numbers are, the typical cost to educate a vocational-technical student is $16,000 to $17,000 per year, about 35 percent above the $11,000 average cost per student in a Boston Archdiocese high school. Attracting private-sector professionals also requires higher teacher salaries. Frequent upgrades are required to maintain equipment in programs such as advanced manufacturing or heating, ventilation, and air conditioning. Minimum size requirements are needed to comply with student-teacher ratios.

A health assisting program is among the least expensive voc-tech programs, but it's still not cheap:

- At Assabet Valley Regional Technical High School in Marlborough, the fiscal 2017 budget for health technologies was $340,652, according to Superintendent Ernest Houle. About $336,000 of that is for salaries.[323]
- At Bay Path Regional Vocational Technical High School in Charlton, 80 students are in the health assisting program, and salaries for four instructors totaled $338,000 in 2018, according to Superintendent John Lafleche. A new dental program required about $300,000 to outfit the lab. The instructor salary was $61,000.[324]
- Minuteman Regional Vocational Technical High School in Lexington built a new school. Superintendent Edward A.

Bouquillon estimated $10,000 per student for furniture, fixtures and equipment — at least $150,000 for a 15-student program in the first year.[325]

Public vocational-technical schools enjoy taxpayer support and also receive financial aid through the Carl D. Perkins Career and Technical Education grant program, federal money that can be used for staffing and equipment.

Catholic schools receive no public funds and aren't eligible for Perkins grants. Without taxpayer support, Ferreira said it would be unrealistic to expect the Archdiocese to run a similar school, since tuition alone "is not going to be anywhere sufficient enough to provide this kind of school."[326]

Each high school in the Archdiocese raises about $200,000 to $400,000 annually through tuition and fundraising. Tuitions vary widely, and most schools provide financial aid, including discounts for siblings. At Boston College High School, for example, nearly half the students receive assistance, an average of about $8,300 annually.[327]

Along with lower enrollments and declining tuition revenue, Catholic schools have experienced a transition "from a basically free workforce in the persons of religious priests, brothers, and women to one comprised predominantly of the laity, who rightly must receive just wages and benefits," said George Henry, former superintendent of Catholic education for the Archdiocese of St. Louis.[328]

Chris Fay, principal of Christian Brothers High School in Memphis, Tennessee, said schools are struggling to pay reasonable salaries without pricing their schools above what their families can pay.[329]

Cost-Saving Strategies

Even in a relatively low-cost voc-tech discipline such as health assisting, creating lab spaces that meet state specifications is expensive.

"Your facilities need to be a minimum size," Bouquillon said. "If the student-teacher ratio is maxed out at 15, you need at least 1,900 square feet. And if you expect to go into medical laboratory technology, you're going to need a larger shop area."

One cost-saving approach for Catholic schools could be to use the facilities of existing voc-tech schools during the school day or after hours, rather than building their own.

Mears, who was the assistant superintendent of schools at the Archdiocese of Indianapolis, saw such a partnership work in Indiana.

"We sent our kids to the public schools for voc-tech, but they still took their English, math and other core subjects at the Catholic school. The voc-tech loved it because they counted as their students and they got the money from the state for them."

Massachusetts voc-tech superintendents are open to working with Catholic schools, but staffing, scheduling, and financing all need to be worked out.

"If a Catholic school were located near a regional vocational school, there are models that could be used," said Lafleche of Bay Path.

With 40 weeks in a school year, he said it would be easy to get 300 to 400 hours in after school.

Bouquillon said he's committed to working with traditional schools, private schools, and charter schools. The caveat is whether the district offering a voc-tech program would be allowed to count each student and be compensated by the Commonwealth.

Lexington High School students who have passed MCAS may attend the "Minuteman in the Morning" program and return to Lexington High for the remainder of the school day. They earn a diploma from Lexington High School and a certificate from Minuteman.

Creating a Voc-Tech Program

A health services program could fit well with the Boston-area economy, with its many hospitals and employment opportunities in health care, especially for low-income students.

"If kids who are economically disadvantaged can complete some kind of certificate program in the time they graduate from high school, then they will have a job that will probably pay between $30,000 and $40,000," says Mears. "It could be a total game changer for economically disadvantaged children."

But the Archdiocese faces a tall task if it commits to adding a voc-tech program.[330] Under Chapter 74 of the state laws, public schools proposing CVTE programs must demonstrate a need for and student interest in a program, and that the program will prepare students for high-wage, high-need jobs.

Catholic high schools are not required to comply with Chapter 74 regulations because they are private. But any voc-tech program in health services needs to be competitive with other schools in that space.

"If School X has 1,000 students, the only way a program like this makes sense is if now you have 1,020 students, because 20 of them came specifically for this program," said Lafleche of Bay Path. "If the tuition is $10,000 per year, there's an extra $200,000 to work with. So, if you're going to put this program in the high school and not grow your population, you're adding a heck of a lot of cost with no revenue."

When students graduate from a health assisting program, they typically hold one or more of several industry-recognized credentials, such as a Nurse Assistant certification (CNA), first aid certification, a license to operate an EKG machine, an EMT license, and perhaps a phlebotomy license. By preparing students in the allied health fields, the Archdiocese would give them an advantage in college admissions into STEM fields.

For instance, for a student who wants to be a pharmacist (current average salary $115,000), what better background for admittance into the Massachusetts College of Pharmacy and Health Sciences' Doctor of Pharmacy program than a pharmacy technician certificate? A certified background in an allied health or nursing field is a tremendous asset for any serious applicant.[331]

CVTE high schools in Massachusetts have proven that voc-tech and college prep can be combined. Many students take AP and honors courses and go to college. But major differences remain. While Catholic school teachers are not required to be licensed by the DESE, anyone teaching in a health-related voc-tech program, public or private, must be licensed in medical areas — although there is a grace period.

"During the first year when you're operating as a non-CTE you can have a teacher with just a science background teaching it," said Victoria Kelly, career academy coordinator at Haverhill High School. "We had a biotech teacher who taught it the first year. But in order to get vocationally certified for health assisting we need an RN."[332]

Voc-tech programs must meet state-mandated teacher/student ratios. And, unlike college prep students, voc-tech schools generally split their time each day between the classroom and the clinical instruction that is one of the foundational components of the voc-tech experience.

Further, health disciplines require some clinical affiliation in which a nurse goes with students to do hands-on care. While freshman and sophomores have mock training in the laboratory, Ferreira said that students "have hands-on experience with actual patients as they become juniors and seniors."

Students must record a minimum of 120 hours of lab work to qualify for a CNA (and pass an exam), but it's not unusual for teenagers to take longer to be trained and ready for the test.

Mercy Career & Technical High School

Mercy Career & Technical High School in Philadelphia is the nation's only coed Catholic CVTE high school. It proves that voc-tech can work for a Catholic school, but also demonstrates that it might take unique circumstances to pay for it.

Founded in 1950 by the Sisters of Mercy as a three-year certificate technical school, Mercy converted into a full high school in the 1970s. It prepares graduates for continuing education or immediate employment. Students earn a high school diploma and study to achieve industry-recognized certifications in their chosen career and technical program.

In addition to a standard academic program, Mercy has six career technical education programs: business, building trades, computer technology, cosmetology, culinary arts, and nurse aide training.

Freshmen take a career exploration course of one period per week, which helps them make their career and technical program decisions at the end of that year. They take the CVTE curriculum for the next three years and may participate as seniors in the school's co-op program. Mercy reports 99 percent graduation and 97 percent attendance rates.[333]

Much like Catholic high schools in Boston, tuition alone could not support the CVTE program at Mercy. Tuition is $8,400, but the cost to educate each student is $12,500, and more than 90 percent of Mercy's students qualify for assistance.[334]

As a private school, Mercy does not receive state taxpayer funds, federal Perkins Grant money, or an allowance from the Archdiocese of Philadelphia. But Mercy does benefit from state tax laws and agreements.

In 2016, the school raised more than $1.86 million in gifts, including $353,500 received through Pennsylvania's Educational Improvement Tax Credit (EITC) and Opportunity Scholarship Tax Credit (OSTC) programs, which extend tax credits to businesses contributing to scholarship organizations.

In the 2015–2016, 48 Mercy families received tuition assistance through the EITC and nearly 100 families through the OSTC.[335]

Since 1992, Mercy has also shared in an annual $1.5 million fund from the Pennsylvania Convention Center. In 2016, Mercy's gift of $278,667 financed core training in the building trades, business education, and culinary arts.

Mercy's Nurse Aide Training Program (NATP) prepares students for health careers over a period of three academic years. At the end of their junior year, students qualify to take the Pennsylvania Nurse Aide Certification examination.[336]

"We're looking to add more to that program," said Catherine Glatts, vice principal of technology and career and technical education. "We could teach medical coding and medical assistance. Those aren't expensive. Our nursing is long-term care. We're looking to also bring in acute care."

Mercy partners with local businesses and others for materials and co-op opportunities. In 2016, Local 98 of the International Brotherhood of Electrical Workers (IBEW) donated materials that Mercy students could not afford. In return, the IBEW and other partners use Mercy's facilities during after-school hours.

Conclusion

Leaders of Archdiocese of Boston high schools face challenging times. Enrollment has fallen at many of its schools and the allure of a college-prep high school has faded as many college graduates struggle to get jobs. More families are turning to a career voc-tech education so their children can graduate with employable skills and a solid foundation for higher education.

In response, Catholic high schools are considering breaking from tradition to incorporate voc-tech education. The preferred discipline would be health care, given the enormous employment based that exists in metropolitan Boston.

But the money issue is still significant. Tuition revenue is inadequate to cover costs, fundraising income varies among the 30 high schools, and the Archdiocese of Boston does not provide any financial assistance.

A study has been commissioned by the Catholic Schools Office to help determine if there is a strong enough demand among families of prospective students to add voc-tech to the curriculum.

Recommendations
Repeal Massachusetts's two Anti-Aid Amendments

As recommended earlier in this book, repeal of Anti-Aid or Know-Nothing Amendments to the Massachusetts Constitution is essential to helping close the enormous difference between the ability of Massachusetts's regional career vocational technical education schools to offer programs and that of Catholic high schools to do so. The Supreme Court of the United States decision in *Espinoza v. Montana Department of Revenue* may not directly affect the state's Anti-Aid Amendment, but it provides encouragement for the Commonwealth to head in that direction.

Explore a partnership between the Archdiocese and regional public CVTE schools

Startup costs, even for relatively low-budget health care programs, can run into the hundreds of thousands of dollars. Regional CVTE superintendents are open to cooperation with Catholic high schools. Catholic school voc-tech students could split their day between a public CVTE school and their Catholic high school. Using public school facilities would enable Catholic schools to begin a CVTE program while creating their own lab space in a way that is financially feasible.

Investigate start-up assistance organizations

To mitigate startup costs, school could turn to licensed organizations that handle the heavy lifting for a school that wants to add nursing and allied health programs. For a flat rate of up to $20,000, for example, Kaduceus, Inc. sells packages for a class of 25, including textbooks, classroom and lab supplies, online assessments, teacher guides, and up to five days of free training to one instructor. Setting up new programs is a huge commitment, but using proven programs can get the process going very quickly.

Meet Chapter 74 requirements

Catholic high schools are not required to meet state Chapter 74 standards for voc-tech education, but would be more competitive if they did. The "Chapter 74 Manual for Vocational Technical Education Programs," published by the Massachusetts DESE, is a resource for school districts in the implementation of voc-tech programs.

Alison Fraser is an education policy, research, and strategy consultant and president of Practical Policy. Previously, she was an administrator at Blackstone Valley Tech and director of policy and advocacy at Mass Insight Education, where she directed the Great Schools Campaign and development of No Excuses for Failing Schools and Excellence in Math and Science Goals. An expert in standards-based curriculum, Fraser has coordinated activities and programs for the Coalition for Higher Standards and led research in standards-based reform.

William Donovan is a former staff writer with the *Providence Journal* in Rhode Island, where he wrote about business and government. He has taught business journalism in the graduate programs at Boston University and Northeastern University. He received his undergraduate degree from Boston College and his Master's in Journalism from American University in Washington, D.C.

Chapter 8: No IDEA: How Massachusetts Blocks Federal Special Education Funding for Private and Religious School Students

By Tom Olson, Steve Perla & William Donovan

Executive Summary

For at least 14 years, thousands of Massachusetts children have been denied the special education services to which they are entitled under federal civil rights law. The issue came to a head in 2019, when the U.S. Department of Education (USED) found that the Commonwealth has been violating federal IDEA law for over a decade. While the state has taken some steps to remedy past wrongs, well over $100 million is at stake for children who were denied the special education services to which they are entitled, and it may take further litigation to resolve years of injustice.

This chapter examines why this state of affairs has persisted for so long and offers recommendations that could correct these wrongs that so negatively impact thousands of private school students in the Commonwealth.

Introduction & Background

Like many private school children, Denny is a gifted child who also has special needs. To Denny's parents, it is extremely important that he attend the same Catholic school as his siblings.

A valued part of their parish community, the school also possesses a mission that comports well with the values that they, as parents, want to pass on to *all* their children.

Denny's mother wrote: "Like his older sister, Denny is enrolled in a suburban Catholic elementary school in our hometown. Concerns about Denny's academic progress began in kindergarten. He was lagging behind his classmates in alphabet memorization and was unable to recite numeric order past the number 13. The decision was made, however, to promote him to Grade 1 with hopes that it was just developmental.

In reality, Grade 1 proved to be more difficult and the academic gap widened. Anxiety set in, and a happy little six-year-old showed early signs of depression. Through much perseverance, however, Denny made sufficient progress to be promoted to Grade 2.

Within the first few months of Grade 2, Denny was again falling behind rapidly. The other students were now reading, while Denny was still struggling with phonics. Within a few months, Denny was examined by a neurologist and diagnosed with dyslexia. It was recommended that he receive specialized instruction in the area of reading."[337]

In the not-too-distant past it was a struggle for children such as Denny with learning disabilities to receive the same educational opportunities as other children. This was a struggle that both public school *and* private school children endured. As late as 1970, American schools educated only one in five children with disabilities. Many states excluded from public school certain students who were "deaf, blind, emotionally disturbed, or mentally retarded."[338]

In 1975, Congress passed the *Education for All Handicapped Children Act*. At that time, nearly 1.8 million children with disabilities had been excluded from receiving an education that addressed their special needs.

In 1990, the name of this act changed to the *Individuals with Disabilities Education Act* (IDEA). IDEA requires each state to ensure that all eligible public and private school children with disabilities receive a free and public education.[339] As a result, more than 6.9 million children with disabilities now receive special education and related services.

Rather than being warehoused in a separate location, more than 62 percent of these children are now enrolled in general education classrooms during 80 percent or more of their school day. Furthermore, early intervention services are being provided to more than 340,000 infants and toddlers with disabilities.[340]

Each year, the federal government allocates billions in IDEA dollars to the states, which in turn apportion their respective federal allocations to their local education agencies (LEAs).[341] In fiscal year 2018, Massachusetts received more than $255.5 million in IDEA funds for both public and private school students.[342]

The IDEA law includes comprehensive guidelines on how private school students' allocations and services should be determined. Among the guidelines are specific directives on how LEAs are to collaborate with private schools to make and finalize the determinations. Chief among those means of determination is a process that the law calls "Child Find." Each LEA is obligated to test any child who is suspected by his or her parents of having one or more disabilities. This applies to students attending a private school within the LEA, whether or not the students reside within the LEA.

The Key Role of 'Proportionate Share'

The LEA must also hold "timely and meaningful" meetings among private school officials, private school parents, and LEA officials. These consultation meetings determine "how, where, and by whom special education and related services will be provided."[343]

However, before any positive and impactful conclusions about these matters can come from these consultation meetings, a matter called "proportionate share" must first be determined. This matter is incredibly important to private school students and their families because, unlike their public-school counterparts, private school students do not receive IDEA services as an individual entitlement.

Rather, the private school students who qualify for special education services in any given LEA attain, collectively, a "proportionate share"[344] of the total IDEA funds that the federal government has allocated to that particular LEA. Unlike their public-school counterparts who each have a guaranteed individual entitlement to IDEA services, private school children are granted a "group entitlement." This means that not all special needs children will receive services.

The Massachusetts Department of Elementary and Secondary Education (DESE) failed to provide proper guidance to LEAs about the "proportionate share" process. This was due to DESE's mistaken application of the Commonwealth's Anti-Aid or Blaine Amendment,[345] enshrined within Article XVIII of the state Constitution,[346] which completely disallows public aid to private schools.

State legislation provides private school students the opportunity to access state and locally funded special education services that "...shall be comparable in quality, scope, and opportunity for participation to that provided to public-school students with needs of equal importance."[347]

However, DESE has interpreted the Blaine Amendment to mean that special education services provided with state and local funds cannot be provided on private school grounds. Instead, these services may be offered at public schools or a "neutral" location. As a matter of practice, services are *only* offered at public schools, and the public school at which the services are offered is the school located in the municipality in which the student *resides*.

For example, a student who resides in Sharon and attends a private school in Brookline would have to travel back to Sharon to receive services. Publicly funded transportation for such travel is not offered. This means that if special needs children are to receive the state-funded special education services to which they are entitled, both those children's school day and their parents' workday must constantly be interrupted. Children must miss precious instructional time in their own classrooms. Parents must take time off from work. This is an untenable situation that places impossible demands upon them.

It is important to remember that the parents of special needs children who choose to send their children to private schools generally pay similar amounts in federal taxes as public-school parents. Despite this, and for the two reasons presented above, parents who choose to send their special needs children to private schools must make a difficult choice between assenting to their children not receiving special education services or paying out-of-pocket for those services.

A Faulty Application of Special Education Laws

One might wonder how a state that so prides itself on its educational system can justify this. Ironically, the Commonwealth does so by pointing to its own special education laws and assuming that those laws are both *de facto* and *de jure* more generous to private school children with special needs than those provided to them under federal law (IDEA). Nothing could be further from the truth.

Seventeen percent of students in Massachusetts's public schools receive special education services, whereas *less than 1 percent* of private school students do.[348] The primary reason for this lamentable reality is the state's requirement that private school students with disabilities must receive special education services at local public schools rather than on their private school campuses.

In the name of avoiding any actual or perceived support of private schools, DESE denies services to private school children notwithstanding their entitlement to receive such support.

Denny's mother feared that it might be next to impossible for her to both send Denny to the private school that she and her husband wanted for him *and* ensure that he would be able to receive the special education services he needed. She wrote: "It was recommended that he receive specialized instruction in the area of reading. Attending a Catholic elementary school with very little special education services, we were heartbroken knowing the possibility that Denny may have to leave this school to attend a local public school."

Advocacy: Round 1

In 2007, representatives from the Parents Alliance for Catholic Education (PACE) and the Bureau of Jewish Education of Greater Boston (BJE) proposed amending state private school special education regulation 603 CMR 28:03 so private school students could receive, at their respective private schools, state and locally funded special education services.

To avoid proposing a change that would run afoul of Massachusetts's Anti-Aid Amendment, PACE and BJE suggested to the Commonwealth that state and locally funded services be allowed on-site at their schools in a "neutral location," defined as any room or space on the grounds of private schools that are devoid of any religious symbolism. PACE and BJE went so far as to define a neutral location as rooms that would be used *exclusively* for special education services. State officials rejected this proposal.

The associate commissioner of DESE wrote, "[t]he Department adopted [603 CMR 28:03] with explicit reference to private schools, public schools, and neutral sites to avoid any constitutional problems under the Anti-Aid Amendment of the Massachusetts Constitution." The associate commissioner added that allowing "certain limited services" on-site, as the private schools were requesting, would likely draw legal challenges under the Anti-Aid Amendment.

"Special education," the associate commissioner wrote, "is a continuum of services providing access to the general education curriculum. Many types of special education services are more directly related to general instruction and would become impermissibly intertwined with the private school program in violation of the Anti-Aid Amendment."[349]

How, we ask, could secular special education services provided in a room set aside exclusively for this purpose "become impermissibly intertwined with the private school program?"

Advocacy: Round 2

In 2015, the private school coalition—now including PACE and two organizations representing Jewish private school children—decided on a shift in strategy. Prompting this shift was the vision and leadership of the Ruderman Family Foundation and the fact that, according to the IDEA law, private school students with special needs have a right to their share of IDEA-funded services.

For example, if an LEA has 100 students with disabilities, and 10 of them attend private schools, then those students are entitled to 10 percent of the IDEA grant to provide services. Under IDEA, LEAs are encouraged to provide these services to private school students on-site at their private schools unless there is a compelling reason for the services to be offered elsewhere.[350] Massachusetts law also allows for this support to be provided on-site when federal funds are utilized.[351]

"Even if it's a third of the need or a tenth, we could access 100 percent of that third or tenth," said Stephen Perla, Superintendent of Schools for the Roman Catholic Diocese of Fall River. "So that's why we really started to go after the federal law and say to the state, 'What are you doing to make sure our kids access their federal law entitlement?' It turns out the state had completely ignored the federal law entitlement. They had the mistaken assumption that our kids already had access to 100 percent of services and therefore they really didn't have to bother with this small federal entitlement."[352]

DESE mistakenly guided LEAs to follow state law, maintaining that the LEAs' federal law obligations under IDEA could be met by complying with Massachusetts's special education law. LEAs were careful to follow the state law and offer services to students who could access them at public schools. At the same time, they insisted that services—even those funded with federal dollars—could not be provided on-site at private schools. *De facto*, private school students for the most part could not access even their smaller group entitlement to proportionate share.

At the request of PACE, the U.S. Department of Education's

Office of Special Education Programs (OSEP) reviewed DESE's implementation of IDEA. OSEP's audit determined that the Commonwealth did *not* have procedures in place to "ensure that (LEAs) spend the required amount of their (IDEA grants) on providing special education and related services to parentally-placed private school children with disabilities in accordance with the requirements..."

OSEP directed DESE to take corrective actions.

In June 2017, DESE sent a memo to all LEAs in which the calculation requirements for proportionate share were outlined. They asked the LEAs to recalculate their proportionate shares for the 2016–17 and 2017–18 school years. The memo clarified that each LEA must *also* include in its respective proportionate share determination private school children who reside outside of the LEA but attend private schools within it.

"The state's clarification was shock and awe, to be honest with you," said Elizabeth O'Connell, director of special education for Dedham Public Schools. "I didn't write the IEP for the (out-of-town) student going to a private school in Dedham. But because that school happens to be in Dedham, I have some ownership for implementing that IEP. I don't have to ensure a free and appropriate public education, but I have to allocate some of our public funds to supporting that student. That's very much new information in Massachusetts."[353]

Lisa Moy, executive director of special education for the Fall River Public Schools, has been working to improve the accuracy of the count of private school special education students in the Fall River LEA. She suspects that in the past, the count was inaccurate and unmaintained because LEAs had not been asked by DESE to monitor the Child Find data.

Moy said that she regrets that DESE has caused—or not prevented—confusion among the ranks. "I think that's where the misguidance has come from with the state."[354]

Hoping the state would realize the error of its ways and do right by the private school children who had been denied special education services for so long, a coalition of Catholic and Jewish schools requested and conducted a series of meetings with senior leaders of DESE, in hopes that IDEA would finally be promptly and properly implemented. But after two years of meetings, nothing had changed.

Despite assurances and promises and commitments, private school children with disabilities were still being denied the services to which they were entitled. No one agent or representative of the Commonwealth was explicitly responsible for this failure. However, complacency, complicity, inattentiveness, and, in some cases, hostility toward the notion that private school children with special needs are as deserving of services as their public-school counterparts coalesced to thwart change.

Advocacy: Round 3

Thus, in June 2017, the private school coalition filed 26 complaints. Of these, 25 were against LEAs throughout the Commonwealth; one was against DESE, through its "Problem Resolution System (PRS)," part of the DESE's "Program Quality Assurance Services." According to the complaints, DESE identified *only* 894 private school students who received special education services from their home LEAs, or less than 1 percent of all students in the state who are enrolled in private schools.

From their own survey of approximately 10,000 of their students, however, private school leaders discovered that 16 percent[355] required special education services.[356] Only one conclusion could be drawn: Private school students with special needs were not being counted and were not receiving their "proportionate share" of IDEA services.

The complaint added: "Even if we use a lower number and assume, for example, that only five percent of the private school population in Massachusetts has special education needs, the proportionate share allocation would jump to $8,646,373. DESE, through its failure to have policies and procedures in effect to ensure that the LEAs correctly calculate and spend proportionate share and its failure to monitor LEAs expenditures, has committed major violations of IDEA, with the result that private school students have been deprived for years of equitable services that Congress intended them to receive."[357]

Using DESE's 2014–15 published number of parentally placed private school students, together with the published IDEA allocation for the same academic year ($247.75 million), and assuming that 16 percent of the total school population (more than 955,000 students) have special education needs, private school students would make up only 0.58 percent of the total population of students with special education needs. That would mean just $1.44 million would need to be spent on services for them.

However, assuming the data we have gathered holds true for the rest of the private school population, some 16 percent of the more than 110,000 private school students statewide have special needs. By that calculation, private school students would account for just over 10 percent of students with disabilities in Massachusetts. The proportionate share allocation would consequently rise to $25.67 million, a difference of more than $24 million.[358]

In March 2017, DESE and private school officials met to review new data from DESE on eligible private school students from the 2015–2016 school year. According to the private schools' complaint to PRS, at that time only 212 LEAs had been surveyed, but the number of private school students had jumped from an earlier number of 894 to 1,715. Private school officials said the discrepancy was further evidence that DESE was neither monitoring LEA record keeping nor ensuring that they were accurately counting private school students with disabilities.

Limiting its investigation to the one-year period preceding the coalition's filing of its complaint, PRS found, in response to the filed complaint:[359]

- DESE did not fully implement regulatory requirements relating to consultations between private school representatives and LEAs.

- DESE only partially corrected its noncompliance with record-keeping requirements by issuing a memorandum to LEAs.

- DESE only partially corrected its noncompliance with regulatory requirements relating to calculation and expenditure of proportionate share of IDEA funds following the OSEP audit.

PRS next issued a letter directing DESE to take corrective actions and each LEA received a letter regarding its noncompliance. However, the PRS did not detail for each LEA the specifics of its noncompliance or necessary corrective actions. Instead, a boilerplate remedy was imposed that had no real effect.

As a result, there remain to this day LEAs that are non-compliant. In addition, and as a result of PRS limiting its investigation to the one-year period preceding the coalition's filing of its complaint — PRS failed to make amends for each of the 11 years preceding the investigation period during which private school students did not receive the IDEA-funded services to which they were entitled.

Advocacy: Round 4

In October 2017, the coalition appealed to the U.S. Secretary of Education, alleging PRS improperly limited the scope of its investigations and that the corrective actions ordered were insufficient. The coalition claimed that, over a period of a dozen years, between $96 million and $290 million of IDEA funds allocated to the Commonwealth's LEAs should have been used to serve private school students. The coalition requested compensatory services from the LEAs and DESE.[360]

The private school coalition's ultimate goal is for private school children to have real and meaningful access to the special education services to which they are entitled under both state and federal (IDEA) law. If the Commonwealth would follow both the letter and the spirit of the laws, this goal could be achieved.

The reasoned application of state law to a real-world situation proves this point vis-à-vis state law.

Aaron is a student with dyslexia who attends a Jewish day school. Unlike many children, Aaron just happens to be lucky enough to have a stay-at-home parent who, three days a week, is able to transport him to his hometown's public school.

On each of those three days, Aaron leaves his private school right after lunch to go to his hometown's public school, where he is able to receive services essential to his academic success and emotional well-being. This allows Aaron's parents to keep him with his siblings in a school community that is important to his self-esteem and reinforces his family's values.

However, three days a week, Aaron misses up to a period and a half of valuable class time and the opportunity to play and socialize with his peers at recess. This arrangement could have lasting negative effects on his overall educational and social formation.

For now, Massachusetts's special education laws allow for state funds to be used to provide special education for private school students on public school grounds. This is not deemed a violation of the Blaine Amendment. But if children such as Aaron and Denny were to receive special education services at their private schools, thus removing the logistical barriers outlined above, would receiving these services violate state law?

Although never formally considered by Massachusetts courts, the United States Supreme Court has held that special education services provided on-site at private schools would not violate the First Amendment of the United States Constitution.[361] The coalition believes the same analysis could be extended to Article XVIII of the Massachusetts Constitution.

The coalition's thinking on this is informed by Massachusetts case law. But in 1978, the Supreme Judicial Court of Massachusetts ruled that a school committee's loaning of textbooks to pupils attending private schools violated the Anti-Aid Amendment.[362] The court found that although the textbooks were provided directly to the students, loaning the textbooks constituted "substantial aid" to the private school. The court distinguished between textbooks and "other sundry general benefits not entering into the educational process," such as health services, student nutrition programs, and transportation.

But four years later, the Essex County Superior Court saw things differently. The town of Essex argued on the basis of the Anti-Aid Amendment that it should not be required to provide transportation to residents attending a private school.[363] Here, the court found that transportation was a public safety measure similar to fire and police protections. Since transportation was provided directly to students and conferred only a remote benefit on the private school, it did not violate the Anti-Aid Amendment.

In light of this ruling and the Massachusetts Supreme Judicial Court's recent affirmation of this three-part test,[364] how can DESE continue to hold that the location of services, provided directly to and consumed entirely by a student, determines whether these services are *required* or *forbidden* by state law? Could it really be that the same services provided to the same student by the same staff member in one location are permitted and deemed to solely benefit the student, but that in another location those same services are deemed "substantial aid" to the school itself?

After the 2017 publication of the paper from which this chapter is derived, the United States Department of Education found that the Commonwealth was in violation of federal law. In 2019, advocates estimated that as much as $120 million could be owed to private schools for the failure of the state to enforce a federal law requiring local districts to share IDEA funding with children in all schools, including religious schools. Those monies would come in the form of services that districts are required to provide to private school students. In the meantime, the Commonwealth has taken steps to emphasize federal law and guidance (rather than state law) on matters of special education and proportionate share.

Conclusions and Recommendations

Aaron's case, when analyzed against the above-presented three points, yields the following conclusions:

- Aaron's receipt of state-funded special education services on-site at his private school would redound to his educational benefit and not to the financial benefit — or any other quantifiable benefit — of his private school.
- Aaron's receipt of religiously neutral services on-site at his private school, by district staff members or contractors in a thoroughly non-sectarian space, would be for all intents and purposes "remote."

- Aaron's receipt of said services to which the law entitles him would have no direct financial impact on the LEA, which is already obligated by state law to provide services to resident students, like Aaron, regardless of whether they attend public or private school.

In light of all this, the private school coalition offers the following recommendations:

- The Massachusetts State Board of Elementary and Secondary Education should amend the regulation that prevents the use of state and local funds to deliver special education services to private school students at the private school site.

- A private school special education ombudsman should be appointed to help address systemic issues raised in the private school complaints that have been brought to light over a decade's worth of noncompliance.[365] DESE should take a more active role to ensure that LEAs change the entrenched practice of overlooking private school students with disabilities. Such efforts might include (1) implementing joint training sessions for public and private school leaders to ensure that the message communicated to each group is clear and uniform, and (2) convening a private school working group to meet quarterly to learn of issues in the field.

- DESE should also implement additional reporting requirements to increase transparency and accountability regarding the expenditure of IDEA funds earmarked for private school students. LEAs should be required to publish on a regular basis (1) the amount of funds designated for private school students with disabilities, (2) meeting dates with private school leaders, and (3) an accounting of how the funds were spent.

- DESE should direct the LEAs to spend each private school's federal IDEA dollars on-site at the private school unless there is a compelling reason for services to be provided off-site. If such compelling reasons exist, the LEA must document the reason(s) in writing and still provide transportation for the students.

- DESE should require each LEA to spend IDEA funds generated by students in a particular school on students within that school unless a group of schools within that LEA agree to pool funds. This is consistent with other federal programs that provide for equitable sharing, including Title I.

✼ ✼ ✼

Tom Olson is a Principal Partner of ADAC. A Roman Catholic priest, Olson has overseen development efforts, augmented donor commitment, and cultivated major gifts for a variety of organizations. Supporting initiatives that advance in government and civil society limited government and the principle of subsidiarity, Olson's professional competencies include published writing and public policy research. He holds a Bachelor of Arts from the College of the Holy Cross and graduate degrees from Saint Louis University and Boston College.

Steve Perla is a Principal Partner of ADAC. Over the past 26 years, he has successfully advocated for and obtained over a billion dollars' worth of federally funded education services for non-public schools. He has also advanced and secured the support for key public policy issues such as early education vouchers, school health, and special education services for non-public schools in Massachusetts. Perla has served as a Catholic school superintendent for two dioceses, led the University of Notre Dame's ACE consulting group, and was the founding Executive Director of the Boston-based Parents Alliance for Catholic Education. Perla served 12 years in elective office, including two terms as Mayor of Leominster, Massachusetts. He holds a Bachelor's degree from Lesley University and a Master's degree from Boston College.

William Donovan is a former staff writer with the *Providence Journal* in Rhode Island, where he wrote about business and government. He has taught business journalism in the graduate programs at Boston University and Northeastern University. He received his undergraduate degree from Boston College and his Master's in Journalism from American University in Washington, D.C.

Chapter 9:
Nurturing Faith and Illuminating Lives: Conclusion and Recommendations

By Patrick Wolf, Ph.D.

I start with a confession. I am the product of 16 years of Catholic education. Far from being a sin, Catholic schooling proved to be my salvation, in ways both large and small. I grew up in a single-parent family in St. Cloud, Minnesota. My sisters and I were eligible for free lunches. According to the U.S. Census, given my childhood demographic characteristics, I had a better chance of being incarcerated than of graduating from college.[366]

Fortunately, demographics were not destiny for my sisters and me. In spite of our challenges, we all graduated from college, avoided prison, and have experienced professional success and happy family lives. Throughout our own childhood we benefitted from two luxuries: a loving family and Catholic schooling.

Reading the compelling contributions to this book reminded me of the great gift that a Catholic education has been for me. As George Weigel writes of the educational formation of Pope St. John Paul II, "... the heart of a regenerative culture is its capacity to instill in students a love of learning and a reverence for the truth."[367]

That spirit of truthful inquiry propelled me first through college, as a double-major in philosophy and political science, and then through graduate school, where I completed a doctorate in Government at Harvard University. I like to think that my 16 years of Catholic education nurtured in me "good habits of the heart as well as useful skills and good habits of the mind."[368] Without Catholic schooling, I doubt that I would be contributing to this important work.

The story of Catholic schooling and its past, current, and future contribution to our country is not just about me. It a story of the struggle of an immigrant people to establish a good, and thus godly, life for themselves in a new land of opportunity. It is a story of the commitment to develop the minds, bodies, and souls of the next generation of Americans. It is a tale of initial resistance, struggle, success, and then crisis. It is a story about how Catholic schools have been, and hopefully can continue to be, a lifeline for children from disadvantaged backgrounds such as mine.

In this concluding chapter I highlight salient elements of that story, drawing from vital material in the other chapters of this book, other relevant material, and my own experience of graduating from and then studying Catholic schools. In doing so, I hope to provide a fitting coda to this vital work. I start with a peek at the past and the relevance of that history to today.

The Importance of Catholic Education in America

Until recently, the story of Catholic schooling in the United States was simple. It was a tale of triumph over adversity. That was true about Catholic schooling nationally and especially the case for parochial education in the Commonwealth of Massachusetts.

Catholic parochial schools sprang up in the nineteenth century largely as a response to anti-Catholic bias in the Protestant-themed public schools.[369] As described in painful but vital detail by Cornelius Chapman in Chapter 2, the Know-Nothing political party emerged in the 1840s, primarily in New England, with an agenda to enact laws that, in practice, discriminated against Catholic believers and their institutions.

The poisonous legacy of the Know-Nothings was the Anti-Aid Amendment to the Commonwealth of Massachusetts's Constitution. The provision bans any direct or indirect public aid to "sectarian" organizations. "Sectarian" long has been understood to mean "Catholic," as Protestants view their form of Christianity as a belief system and not a formal "sect" like Catholics do.

Republican Senator James G. Blaine, a one-time nominee for U.S. President, picked up the mantle of anti-Catholic bigotry from the Know-Nothing Party and attempted to enact an amendment to the U.S. Constitution modeled after the Massachusetts Anti-Aid provision. Blaine failed, narrowly, to get that vehicle of anti-Catholic bigotry enshrined in our federal constitution, but he and his followers succeeded in enacting similar amendments, commonly referred to as Blaine Amendments, in 36 states besides Massachusetts.[370]

Although intended initially to prohibit public aid from flowing to Catholic organizations, the Blaine Amendments were eventually interpreted by many courts to proscribe government aid to any pervasively religious organization.

In spite of the headwinds caused by widespread anti-Catholic bigotry and state Blaine Amendments, the Catholic school sector grew throughout the twentieth century, especially after the influx of Italian, German, and Irish immigrants in the second great migration into the U.S., which occurred from 1880 to 1920.

The Ku Klux Klan and other nativist groups succeeded in persuading the Legislature and governor of Oregon to outlaw private schooling, which was overwhelmingly Catholic in the Beaver State, in 1922. The Society of Sisters, an order of teaching Catholic nuns, challenged the constitutionality of the law. In 1925, a unanimous U.S. Supreme Court ruled in favor of the nuns.[371] The Court determined that the Oregon law banning private schooling violated the First Amendment guarantees to parents of freedom of religion and freedom of association, famously declaring that "the child is not the mere creature of the state."

Given the legal protection to operate, Catholic schools thrived in the U.S. through the middle of the twentieth century, reaching their enrollment peak of 5.2 million students, representing over 89 percent of all private school students and 12 percent of all K–12 enrollments, public or private, in 1965.[372] Catholic schools seemed to be in America to stay.

The Catholic School Brand

Repeated charges that Catholic schools are un-American and undermine our democratic republic appear especially bizarre given the Catholic school brand. As Ambassadors Flynn and Glendon eloquently put it in their introduction to this book, throughout American history Catholic schools have sought to implement a vision of "upholding the rule of law, creating compassion for the disadvantaged, and fostering social cohesion."

Catholic school classrooms are known for their crucifixes on the walls and American flags in the corners. The Pledge of Allegiance follows morning prayer and precedes each day's studies. A deep research base confirms that private schools in general, and Catholic schools in particular, produce American citizens who rate higher for tolerance, political knowledge, political activity, and community involvement than their publicly schooled peers.[373]

Economist Julie Trivitt and I have established that U.S. Catholic schools have a brand identity that is easily recognizable to parents. The six elements of the Catholic school brand are 1) consistently high expectations for student learning, 2) a well-ordered, safe and disciplined environment, 3) parental involvement in the school, 4) convenient locations throughout major cities, 5) large class sizes to contain costs, and 6) Christian religious instruction and Catholic worship services in a non-proselytizing spirit.[374]

Ambassadors Flynn and Glendon speak of how the model of Catholic schooling is "a classical liberal arts education that includes religious instruction to aid spiritual development." They point out that, "These schools provide moral and religious education and discipline, characteristics that attract parents of all faiths—nearly 20 percent of students in the Archdiocese of

Boston schools aren't Catholic." The Catholic school brand has served society well.

Current Challenges for Catholic Education

If the previous history of Catholic schooling in America was a straightforward story of success in establishing an attractive educational brand amidst substantial adversity, the recent history of Catholic schools is more complicated. As the chapters in this volume describe in vivid detail, Catholic schools face numerous challenges, including their cost and revenue structures, a decline in middle-class enrollments, a locational mismatch between existing schools and interested clients, the need to provide quality instruction to high-need students, and the recent COVID-19 crisis.

Add to these the pressure to water down the moral messaging that has been central to Catholic schooling for centuries, as well as problematic judicial interpretations of state anti-aid amendments.

I discuss each of these challenges briefly.

Delivering a quality education to students has become increasingly costly in Catholic schools. As detailed by Ambassadors Flynn and Glendon, in the heyday of Catholic schooling in the 1950s and '60s, 75 percent of their faculty and staff were priests, nuns or brothers working for minimal if any compensation. Now, only 4 percent of Catholic school personnel are clerical. Staff salaries compose about 80 percent of the annual cost to educate a child in an Archdiocese of Boston Catholic school, where tuition averages more than $6,500, and the actual cost to educate a child adds as much as $2,000 more to that. The physical infrastructure of many parochial schools is aging and needs repair, but resources are scarce.

Educational resources are much less scarce in the Boston Public Schools (BPS). A recent study that accounts for all of the revenue streams feeding into BPS determined that the public school district received $25,628 in revenue per pupil in fiscal 2018.[375]

Catholic schools in Boston, in contrast, charge families only an average of $2,000 per student in annual tuition. Given costs of more than $6,000 per student, what fills the gap? Previously a combination of school fundraisers, philanthropy, and donations from parishes provided the $4,000 per student subsidy. COVID-19 eliminated most school fundraisers. Philanthropy is stretched thin. The combination of clerical abuse payments and pandemic-induced shutdowns of Masses have wiped out any parish or Archdiocesan financial support for Boston's Catholic schools. The fiscal situation is dire.

One seemingly obvious approach to address the funding gap would be for Catholic schools in the Commonwealth to charge tuitions that more closely approximate the actual costs of educating students. Increasing tuition gives with one hand but takes away with the other. As William Donovan and Jeff Thielman explain in Chapter 5, many middle-class families can barely afford to pay the current, heavily subsidized tuition. Since 1970, "the share of middle-income students attending private schools has declined by almost half, while the private school enrollment rate of wealthy children has remained steady."[376]

Any sharp increase in tuition would drive away more middle-class families, minimizing the subsequent revenue gain because fewer students would be left to pay the higher cost of attending the school.

For over a century, Catholic schools have been concentrated in large cities like Boston that were the gateways for the mass immigration of Catholics from Europe from the 1830s to the 1950s. Fortunately, many immigrant families, including mine, assimilated into the American economy and society in a generation or two and moved from the bowery to small towns and suburbs.

The new communities where second- and third-generation Catholic immigrants lived often lacked Catholic schools but did boast high-quality public schools that were free to enrollees (though funded by state and local taxes) and no longer hostile to Catholics. The need for and availability of Catholic schools was dramatically less for the Catholic families of the urban diaspora.

The result is that Catholic schools now are concentrated in one place, while Catholic families are concentrated in another.

In part because of this locational mismatch, and inspired by the Church's social teachings, urban Catholic schools increasingly serve non-Catholic students with significant educational needs. As George Weigel puts it in the foreword, "Catholic schools must be schools for empowerment." In a certain sense, they have no choice. As Cara Stillings Candal describes vividly in Chapter 1, Catholic schools in the inner city are lifelines for low-income students in desperate need of a quality education. Sadly, the current COVID-19 crisis may result in those lifelines being snapped.

At least 128 Catholic schools in the U.S. have closed permanently as a result of the fiscal emergency visited upon them by the pandemic.[377] Nine of the schools are in the Commonwealth, resulting in over 1,500 students losing access to their Catholic schools.[378] One of the COVID-19 casualties was St. Rose School in Chelsea, Massachusetts, which had operated continuously since 1871. Another closed Catholic school was St. Francis Academy in Bally, Pennsylvania, which was founded in 1743.

Catholic schools that have weathered the storm thus far are actually seeing enrollment increases, as families value their in-person and whole-person approach to educating students amidst the pandemic.[379] Demand for Catholic schooling is increasing even as the supply of Catholic schools is shrinking.

In an effort to attract and maintain tuition-paying families, some Catholic schools are de-emphasizing the moral component of Catholic education, especially regarding sexuality and marriage. We see some evidence of this "watering down" of moral messaging in Catholic schools from surveys of U.S. adults regarding their educational background and marriage outcomes. Although adults who attended Catholic schools during their formative years are 30 percent less likely than otherwise similar public school graduates to have generated a child out of wedlock, they are statistically similar to their public school peers in their likelihood of being in an intact marriage and of never having been divorced.[380]

Adults educated in evangelical Protestant schools, known for promoting stronger messaging regarding sexual morality than many Catholic schools, demonstrate stronger marriage outcomes. Alumni of Protestant schools are more than twice as likely as public school alumni to be in an intact marriage, are 60 percent less likely ever to have been divorced, and are 50 percent less likely to have generated a child out of wedlock. Catholic school leaders should consider the benefits to society and to the Catholic school brand of returning to a clearer and more forceful emphasis on Christian morality in their schools.

The U.S. Supreme Court dealt a potentially fatal blow to anti-aid Blaine Amendments in the 2020 ruling *Espinoza v. Montana Department of Revenue*. Speaking for the Court majority, Chief Justice Roberts wrote, "A State need not subsidize private education. But once a State decides to do so, it cannot disqualify some private schools solely because they are religious."[381]

As Con Chapman discussed in great detail in Chapter 2, Massachusetts is saddled with both an especially restrictive Anti-Aid Amendment and state courts that have interpreted the amendment to be maximally restrictive regarding government aid to private schools. Judicial rulings in the Commonwealth allow funds from the federal government to flow to private schools serving low-income students and students with disabilities, since such support is constitutional according to U.S. Supreme Court rulings.[382] That federal aid to private schools in Massachusetts is a paltry sum, however.

While the *Espinoza* ruling appears to invalidate the claims in several states that state anti-aid amendments require officials to exclude religious schools from receiving government aid supporting the education of children, challenges to practices of religious discrimination in the implementation of private school choice programs in Maine, New Hampshire, and Vermont have yet to be resolved.

Four months after the *Espinoza* ruling, the United States Court of Appeals for the First Circuit ruled that the state of Maine can continue to exclude religious schools from its private school choice program, whereby the state pays the tuition of students who attend private schools in rural areas that lack public schools.[383] State courts in Tennessee have judged a new choice program to be unconstitutional under the Volunteer State's anti-aid amendment.[384]

States continue to use their anti-aid amendments to justify discrimination against private religious schools in the distribution of government aid to education, even though such discrimination clearly violates the Supreme Court ruling in *Espinoza*. Our United States Supreme Court has more work to do to impress upon lower courts and judges that individuals and organizations cannot be denied otherwise available public benefits solely because they are religious.

A Vision for the Future

Catholic schools are facing a potential extinction event in the form of the COVID-19 crisis and its resulting economic shock. The schools that deliver Catholic education across the nation and specifically in Massachusetts will need to evolve in order to survive. The chapters in this book provide a compelling vision for how Catholic schooling needs to adjust going forward.

First, the mix of revenues that support the education of students in Catholic schools needs to change. Catholic schools serve a variety of public interests, including the effective education of students from disadvantaged backgrounds and the inculcation of strong civic values in the next generation of American citizens. Catholic schools cannot continue to produce this bountiful harvest for society while relying exclusively on tuition payments from families, school fundraisers, parish subsidies, and philanthropy. The traditional revenue sources for Catholic schools are being pinched even as the cost of delivering an effective education in Catholic schools is on the rise.

Public funding needs to play a stronger role in supporting the children in Catholic schools. As Ken Ardon and Jason Bedrick argue persuasively in Chapter 4, tax-credit scholarships are a more desirable vehicle for providing new resources to Catholic schools than are school vouchers. Tax-credit scholarships (TCS) are less constitutionally suspect and less prone to overregulation by government than are school vouchers, because TCS do not involve the direct funding of Catholic school students by government. The Florida Tax-Credit Scholarship Program is the largest and, by many accounts, most successful private school choice program in the U.S.[385] It provides an excellent model for providing financial support to needy students in private schools, including Catholic ones.

School choice programs tend to thrive when they are available to a broad swath of low- and middle-income families. A greater quantity and quality of private schools decide to participate in programs with broad student eligibility, providing all qualified families with an extensive and diverse set of private schools from which to choose. Low-income students can be favored in such programs, either by being given a higher-value scholarship or by being given priority in program or school admissions lotteries.

While it is important for Catholic schools to continue their commitment to educating income-disadvantaged students, they only will exist to do so if they can also return many middle-income students to their attendance rolls. The socio-economic diversity of Catholic schools has been an organizational strength. Come, let us all learn together.

Catholic schools must dare to be different from public schools. As Ambassadors Flynn and Glendon state in the introduction, "Catholic schools must resist the public school 'solutions' that would cause them to lose the distinctiveness that attracts families to them in the first place." The temptation to mimic the familiar public-school approach to education, a phenomenon called "institutional isomorphism," is strong.[386] The leaders of Catholic schools need to remember that they are private for a reason and should take advantage of the freedom that private school status bequeaths to them to offer a daringly distinctive alternative to public schools.

Catholic schools also should have the courage to be different from each other. As Cara Candal notes in Chapter 3, while "linked by a common faith," Catholic schools should be "distinct enough from one another to provide high-quality choices for people of diverse backgrounds." Catholic schools should experiment with hybrid homeschooling models and "pandemic pods," expand the availability of Cristo Rey schools, and launch new schools focused on classical education similar to what Pope St. John Paul II experienced in his youth, as George Weigel describes in the foreword.

The unifying elements of a diverse set of Catholic schools should be the application of pedagogically effective learning systems and an emphasis on the core values of Catholicism. Ambassadors Flynn and Glendon capture that vision in the introduction when they describe Catholic education as "a mission to nurture faith and prepare students to live lives illuminated by a Catholic worldview" and to look "for the face of Christ in every person."

Following these guidelines should help America's Catholic schools recapture the middle-class students they are shedding. Public support for Catholic schools in the form of state-based school choice programs will make Catholic schooling more *affordable* to middle- and lower-income American families. Offering a diverse set of distinctive schools, unified in their commitment to Catholic religious and social values, will make Catholic schooling more *attractive* to American middle- and lower-income families. Realizing this vision for Catholic schools will be the great crusade of our time.

Catholic education has deeply shaped my values, principles, aspirations, and character. I am grateful for having had the opportunity to develop my mind, body, and soul in the nurturing environment of a vibrant Catholic elementary school, high school, and college. I close this chapter with a tribute to the many people who made that experience possible for me and so many other Americans. To quote His Holiness, Pope Francis, "Let us thank all those who teach in Catholic schools. Educating is an act of love; it is like giving life."[387]

Patrick Wolf, Ph.D., is the Distinguished Professor of Education Policy and 21st Century Endowed Chair in School Choice in the Department of Education Reform at the University of Arkansas College of Education and Health Professions. He has led or assisted with most of the key evaluations of private school voucher programs over the past 15 years, including recent studies of programs in Washington, D.C., and Milwaukee, Wisconsin, as well as the statewide program in Louisiana. A 1987 graduate of the University of St. Thomas in St. Paul, Minnesota, Dr. Wolf received his Ph.D. in Political Science from Harvard University in 1995.

References

1   Walker Percy, *The Second Coming* (New York: Picador, 1980).

2   Gerard Bradley, Letter to the U.S. Bishops, October 16, 2013.

3   Pope John Paul II, Encyclical Letter, *"Ecclesia de Eucharistia,"* April 17, 2003.

4   Scott W. Hamilton, editor, *Who Will Save America's Urban Catholic Schools?* (New York: Thomas B. Fordham Institute (2008), 7.)

5   NCEA, "United States Catholic Elementary and Secondary Schools 2015-2016: The Annual Statistical Report on Schools, Enrollment, and Staffing."

6   See Cara Stillings Candal, "Be Not Afraid: A History of Catholic Schooling in Massachusetts (Boston: Pioneer Institute, white paper No. 72, March 2011), and https://www.csoboston.org.

7   Ibid.

8   Dr. Mary Grassa O'Neill, Secretary of Education and Superintendent of Schools, Archdiocese of Boston, interview with the author, March 8, 2011; in 2010-11, 18 percent of students in Archdiocese schools did not identify as Catholic.

9   Archdiocese of Boston, Catholic Schools Office (hereafter "AB/CSO"), internal data.

10 Data provided by the Lynch Foundation.

11 See Massachusetts Department of Elementary and Secondary Education (DESE), "Total Expenditure Per Pupil, All Funds, 2018" at http://profiles.doe.mass.edu/statereport/ppx.aspx. Per-pupil costs are much higher in many Massachusetts districts.

12 AB/CSO.

13 See Travis Andersen, "Boston archdiocese schools are in session — with a spike in students," *Boston Globe,* September 10, 2020, and Erin Tiernan, "Catholic schools facing wave of closures amid coronavirus pandemic," *Boston Herald,* August 9, 2020.

14 Charles Glenn, *Myth of the Common School* (Amherst: University of Massachusetts Press, 1988).

15 John J. White, "Puritan City Catholicism: Catholic Education in Boston," in Thomas C. Hunt and Timothy Walch (editors), *Urban Catholic Education: Tales of Twelve American Cities,* Alliance for Catholic Education, Notre Dame, 2010, 92-93.

16 Ibid., 93.

17 Cornelius Chapman, "The Know-Nothing Amendments: Barriers to School Choice in Massachusetts," Pioneer Institute for Public Policy, white paper No. 46, April 2009.

18 Ibid.

19 Ibid.

20 A "system of schools' mentality still exists wherein within parishes fund their own schools and value autonomy. Interviews with Mary Myers, Campaign for Catholic Schools, February 9, 2011, and Monica Haldiman, Sacred Heart School, February 14, 2011.

21 Thomas H. O'Connor, *Boston Catholics: A History of the Church and Its People* (Boston: Northeastern University Press, 1988).

22 White, *Puritan City Catholicism*, 112.

23 O'Connor, *Boston Catholics*, 253.

24 White, *Puritan City Catholicism*, 113, cites Archbishop Cushing as mindful that Catholic school expansion would be unsustainable: "He once stated that he needed to raise $30,000 a day in order to pay for the building that he had been financing — $11 million a year."

25 J. Anthony Lukas, *Common Ground: A Turbulent Decade in the Lives of Three American Families* (New York: Vintage Books, 1986).

26 O'Connor, *Boston Catholics*, 291.

27 AB/CSO, internal data.

28 See demographic data cited in section below, "The Opportunities and Outcomes of Catholic Education."

29 O'Connor, *Boston Catholics*.

30   See Thomas Hoffer, Andrew M. Greeley, and James S. Coleman, "Achievement Growth in Public and Catholic Schools," *Sociology of Education* 58 (2), April 1985, 74-97. The authors find that Catholic school outcomes for minority students are higher than in public schools because Catholic schools "place more students in academic programs, require more semesters of academic coursework, and assign more homework."

31   Anthony Bryk, Valerie Lee, and Peter Holland, *Catholic Schools and the Common Good* (Cambridge: Harvard University Press, 1993).

32   Diane Ravitch, *The Death and Life of the Great American School System*, 127, describes research she commissioned as Assistant Secretary for Education: "I asked my staff to gather information comparing the performance of Hispanic and African American students in Catholic and public schools. I learned that minority kids who attended Catholic schools were more likely to take advanced courses than their peers in public schools, more likely to go to college, and more likely to continue on to graduate school ... I became interested in seeing whether there was any public policy that could sustain these schools."

33   Competition from charter schools is often cited as one reason for Catholic school closings. See Ravitch, *The Death and Life of the Great American School System*, 221.

34   Many of Boston's high-performing charter schools subscribe to a model that has come to be called "No Excuses."

35   Bryk, Lee, and Holland, *Catholic Schools.*

36   Scott Hamilton, ed. *Who Will Save America's Urban Catholic Schools?* Thomas B. Fordham Institute, 2010.

37   See "United States Catholic Elementary and Secondary Schools 2019-2020: The Annual Statistical Report on Schools, Enrollment, and Staffing. Available at ncea.org.

38   See https://www.cato.org/covid-19-permanent-private-closures.

39   Ibid.

40   The Associated Press, "Almost a Dozen Mass. Catholic Schools Closed Amid Pandemic, and Church Warns of More to Come," August 10, 2020. Available at https://www.wbur.org/edify/2020/08/10/a-dozen-mass-catholic-schools-have-closed.

41   See http://www.doe.mass.edu/SchDistrictData.html.

42   Myers, interview.

43   O'Neill, interview.

44   Dr. William McKersie, AB/SCO, interview with the author, January 14, 2011.

45   Although education policies affecting Massachusetts public schools have changed substantially in the late twentieth and early twenty-first century, independent schools are not directly impacted by these reforms. Voucher initiatives to support independent schools have not gained political traction in Massachusetts.

46   See Bryk, Lee, and Holland, *Catholic Schools*, and Ravitch, *The Death and Life of a Great American School System.*

47   See Nan Marie Astone, Sarah S. McClanahan, "Family Structure, Parental Practices, and High School Completion," *American Sociological Review*, 56 (June), 309-320, 1991.

48   Boston Public Schools at a Glance, 2018-2019, available at www.bostonpublicschools.org.

49   Many Catholic and independent schools measure achievement using norm-referenced Terra Nova and Stanford examinations, to compare performance across common curricular content.

50   See https://www.csoboston.org/about/quick-facts.

51   Boston Public Schools at a Glance, 2018-2019, available at www.bostonpublicschools.org.

52   AB/CSO, internal data.

53   Archdiocese data provided by AB/CSO; Boston, state, and national data retrieved from Boston Public Schools at a Glance, 2009-2010, at www.bostonpublicschools.org.

54   AB/CSO, internal data.

55   See http://profiles.doe.mass.edu/statereport/ppx.aspx.

56   See Parental Alliance for Catholic Education (PACE), http://paceorg.net/index.php.

57   Interview with William Leahy, February 1, 2011.

58   AB/CSO, internal data.

59   See Ken Ardon, "Enrollment Trends in Massachusetts," Pioneer Institute Policy Brief, September 2008.

60   See "United States Catholic Elementary and Secondary Schools 2019-2020: The Annual Statistical Report on Schools, Enrollment, and Staffing. Available at ncea.org.

61   McDonald, Dale & Schulz, Margaret, National Catholic Schools Report, 2009-2010: The Annual Report on Schools, Enrollment, and Staffing, The National Catholic Education Association.

62   Leahy, interview.

63   National Catholic Education Association, Catholic School Data, Highlights from The Annual Report on Schools, Enrollment, and Staffing. Available at ncea.org.

64   Myers, Leahy, interviews.

65   Despite accounting for less than 3 percent of the state public school population, four of the 10 best-performing schools on the 2010 MCAS 10th grade math test were charter schools, as were 3 of the top 10 schools in 10th grade English language arts. See: Boston.com, 2010 MCAS results, http://www.boston.com/news/local/breaking_news/2010/09/the_globe_has_c.html.

66   See Ken Ardon, "Enrollment Trends in Massachusetts," 4.

67   According to the Massachusetts DESE Charter School Fact Sheet 2010, charter schools in Massachusetts are roughly 50 percent black and Hispanic. Because students in Archdiocese schools are 73 percent white, it stands to reason that charter schools are not the major reason for enrollment declines in the Archdiocese; but because urban Catholic schools do cater to black and Hispanic students, it is important for them to remain attractive to those populations.

68   See Cara Stillings Candal, "*Debunking the Myths about Charter Public Schools,*" Pioneer Institute Policy Brief, 2010.

69   Leahy, interview.

70   McKersie, interview.

71   Summary Description on Elementary Schools Task Force provided by AB/CSO.

72   McKersie, interview.

73   Interview with Patricia Weisz O'Neill, Roche Center for Catholic Education, Boston College, February 9, 2011.

74   Interviews with O'Brien, McKersie, and Everett.

75   Myers, interview.

76   Hamilton, Scott (Ed.) *Who Will Save America's Urban Catholic Schools?* Thomas B. Fordham Institute, 2010.

77   See Parental Alliance for Catholic Education (PACE), http://paceorg.net/index.php.

78   Among the Archdiocese university partners are Boston College, Regis College, Emmanuel College, and Stonehill College.

79   Bernard Bailyn, *Education in the Formation of American Society* (New York, W.W. Norton, 1972), 11.

80   98 U.S. 145, 162-63 (1879).

81   Massachusetts Constitution, Part 1, Article III.

82   Under the Massachusetts Constitution, a religious taxpayer had some freedom to divert monies; a non-religious taxpayer apparently had no such right.

83   *Gitlow v. New York*, 268 U.S. 652 (1925), is generally considered the first case to so hold. *United States v. Cruikshank*, 92 U.S. 542 (1875), had held to the contrary.

84   Jeff Broadwater, *George Mason: Forgotten Founder* (Chapel Hill: The University of North Carolina Press, 2006), 258, citing P. Slaughter, *The History of Truro Parish in Virginia* (Philadelphia: George W. Jacobs & Company, Publishers), 143-150.

85   Broadwater, 281 citing R. Rutland, *George Mason and the War for Independence* (Williamsburg: Virginia Independence Bicentennial Commission, 57; and R. Rutland, *Mason: Reluctant Statesman* (Baton Rouge: Louisiana State University Press), 68-69.

86   Broadwater, 119-123.

87   Merrill D. Peterson, *Thomas Jefferson: Writings* (New York: The Library of America, 1984), 510 (Letter from Thomas Jefferson to Messrs. Nehemiah Dodge and Others, a Committee of the Danbury Baptist Association in the State of Connecticut, January 1, 1802).

88   Peterson, *Jefferson*, 1465. In a subsequent letter to Dr. Thomas Cooper, Jefferson indicated that the proposed arrangement preserved the various sects' "independence of us and of each other," and would "make the general religion a religion of peace, reason, and morality."

89   Oscar Handlin, *Boston's Immigrants, 1790-1880: A Study in Acculturation* (Cambridge: The Belknap Press of Harvard University Press, 1991), 51-56.

90   For a contemporaneous instance of English anti-Catholicism, see the description of the 1840 "Gordon riots" in Edmund Wilson's *The Wound and the Bow*. Edmund Wilson, Literary Essays and Reviews of the 1930s & 40s (New York: Library of America, 2007), 286.

91   Handlin, 201.

92   Massachusetts Constitution Amendment XVIII, with further amendments by Amendment XLVI and Amendment CIII.

93   Massachusetts Constitution, Part 1, Article III.5

94   Handlin, 168, (citing Official Catholic Yearbook, 1928, 407). The Archdiocese of Boston did not do so until 1884.

95   David O'Brien, *Public Catholicism: Bicentennial History of the Catholic Church in America* (New York: Macmillan Publishing Company, 1989), 47.

96   Debates in the Massachusetts Constitutional Convention 1917-1919 (Boston: Wright & Potter Printing Co.), 90 [hereinafter 1917 Debates] (Debate of John W. Cummings of Fall River).

97   1853 Debates, 621 (Debate of Benjamin F. Butler of Lowell).

98   1917 Debates, 107, 186-7 (Debate of Horace I. Bartlett of Newburyport).

99   J. Anthony Lukas, *Common Ground: A Turbulent Decade in the Lives of Three American Families*, (New York: Random House, 1986), 58.

100   Opinion of the Justices to the Senate and the House of Representatives, 214 Mass. 599 (1913). In the same opinion, three of seven justices took the position that the Anti-Aid Amendment did not prohibit appropriations in aid of churches or religious denominations.

101   1917 Debates, *184-185*. The so-called "anti-sectarian" amendment was introduced in 1900, the year after $10,000 was made to Carney Hospital, a Catholic institution. From 1860 to 1917, nearly $38 million in appropriations had been made for non-Catholic, primarily Protestant institutions.

102   1917 Debates, 212 (Debate of John W. Cummings of Fall River).

103   1917 Debates, 92 (Debate of John W. Cummings of Fall River).

104 1917 Debates, 130 (Debate of Martin Lomasney of Boston, quoting a Protestant named Mr. Parkman whose institution had been receiving $50,000 a year in state aid).

105 1917 Debates, 293.

106 1917 Debates, 290 (Debate of Edwin U. Curtis of Boston quoting John W. Cummings of Fall River).

107 In 1875, Representative James G. Blaine proposed an amendment to the U.S. Constitution to bar aid to sectarian schools; the measure passed the House 180-7 but fell four votes short in the Senate. Steven K. Green, "The Blaine Amendment Reconsidered," 36 *American Journal of Legal History*, 38 (1992).

108 *See, e.g., Hale v. Everett*, 53 N.H. 9, 111 (1868) ("Our fathers were not only Christians; they were, even in Maryland by a vast majority, elsewhere almost unanimously, Protestants," quoting Bancroft's History U.S. 456). *See also* E.I.F. Williams, *The Life of Horace Mann: Educational Statesman* (New York: Macmillan, 1937), 266.

109 1917 Debates, 187 (Debate of Joseph C. Pelletier of Boston).

110 Attorney General v. School Committee of Essex, 387 Mass. 326, 332-33 (citing Everson v. Board of Education of the Township of Ewing, 330 U.S. 1 (1947)).

111 Board of Education of Central School District No. 1 v. Allen, 392 U.S. 236 (1968).

112 See, e.g., *Bloom v. School Committee of Springfield*, 376 Mass. 35 (1978); *Espinoza v. Montana Department of Revenue*. However, the viability of these cases is doubtful in light of *Espinoza* 591 U.S.___ (2020).

113 Massachusetts Constitution, Part 1, Article II (worshipping God according to conscience); Part 1, Article III (all religious sects and denominations enjoy equal protection of the law); Amendment XLVI §1 (No law shall be passed prohibiting the free exercise of religion).

114 530 U.S. 793 (2000).

115 Ibid., 828-29, citing Green, "The Blaine Amendment Reconsidered," 36 *American Journal of Legal History*, 38 (1992).

116 Compare *Reitman v. Mulkey*, 387 U.S. 369 (1967) and *Gordon v. Lance*, 403 U.S. 1 (1971).

117 517 U.S. 620 (1996).

118 Ibid., 634.

119 Ibid., 635, citing *Department of Agriculture v. Moreno*, 413 U.S. 528, 534 (1973); *Kadrmas v. Dickinson Public Schools* 487 U.S. 450, 462 (1988).

120 Ibid., 633.

121 Massachusetts Constitution, Article XLVIII, Part II §2.

122 *Washington v. Glucksberg*, 521 U.S. 702, 721 (1997).

123 *Lochner v. New York* is a leading case from the early days of substantive due process jurisprudence. During the "Lochner Era," roughly 1890 to 1937, economic regulations were routinely overturned on substantive due process grounds. 198 U.S. 45 (1905).

124 See, *e.g., Moore v. City of East Cleveland*, 431 U.S. 494 (1977), in which substantive due process rights overturned a municipal housing ordinance. See also *Roe v. Wade*, 410 U.S. 113 (1973).

125 268 U.S. 510 (1925).

126 Ibid., 534-35.

127 Such as a proficiency test to receive a state certificate of minimum educational attainment.

128 536 U.S. 639, at 676.

129 347 U.S. 483 (1954).

130 Massachusetts Department of Elementary & Secondary Education.

131 Figures for Saint John Paul II Catholic Academy, see https://www.sjp2ca.org/.

132 See maldencatholic.org and www.catholicmemorial.org/admissions/tuition-and-financial-aid.

133 *Attorney General v. School Committee of Essex*, 387 Mass. 326, 332-33 (1982).

134 536 U.S. at 648.

135 2008 Massachusetts Acts, Chapter 182.

136 *Commonwealth v. School Committee of Springfield*, 382 Mass. 665 (1981).

137 *Attorney General v. School Committee of Essex*, 387 Mass. 326 (1982).

138 *Fifty-One Hispanic Residents of Chelsea v. School Committee of Chelsea*, 421 Mass. 598 (1996).

139 See, *e.g.*, Massachusetts General Laws, Chapter 30B, §1(a) (2008).

140 *Lawrence v. Texas*, 539 U.S. 558, 576-577 (2003).

141 See, *e.g.*, General Assembly Resolution ¶7, 1386 (XIV) (Nov. 20, 1959) (United Nations' Declaration of the Rights of the Child).

142 Charles L. Glenn, *The Myth of the Common School* (Oakland, ICS Press, 2002), 270 (quoting Alain Madelin, *Pour libérer l'école: L'enseignement à la carte* (Paris: Laffont, 1984), 176).

143 Adam Smith, *The Wealth of Nations* (Chicago: The University of Chicago Press, 1976), 165.

144 163 U.S. 537 (1896).

145 John T. McGreevey, *Parish Boundaries: The Catholic Encounter With Race in the Twentieth Century Urban North* (Chicago: University of Chicago Press, 1998), 11.

146 Archdiocese of Boston, internal data.

147 Ibid.

148 Data provided by Archdiocese of Boston, Catholic Schools Office (AB/CSO).

149 Data from AB/CSO.

150 See Andy Smarick and Kelly Robson, *Catholic School Renaissance: A Wise Giver's Guide to Strengthening a National Asset* (Washington, D.C.: The Philanthropy Roundtable, 2015), 21. See https://www.philanthropyroundtable.org/docs/default-source/guidebook-files/catholic_schools_interactive_rev.pdf?sfvrsn=f7aba740_0.

151 See website of The Catholic Schools Foundation at https://www.csfboston.org/meet-csf/.

152 See https://www.campaignforcatholicschools.org/about/mission-history.

153 Stephanie Saroki and Christopher Levenick, *Saving America's Urban Catholic Schools* (Washington, D.C.: The Philanthropy Roundtable, 2010), 13-14.

154 Thomas H. O'Connor, *Boston Catholics: A History of the Church and its People* (Boston: Northeastern University Press, 1998).

155 "St. Mary's School in Lawrence to close," *The Boston Pilot*, April 15, 2011.

156 Cynthia Boyle, interview with the author, January 17, 2012.

157 "Archdiocese of Boston breaks new ground with Pope John Paul II Academy," *The Boston Globe*, May 7, 2008.

158 Data provided by Lawrence Catholic Academy and Trinity Catholic Academy.

159 Sister Lucy Veilleux, interview with the author, January 18, 2012.

160 Unpublished position paper provided by Trinity Catholic Academy, Brockton. See https://www.trinitycatholicacademybrockton.org/content/164.

161 Interview with Cynthia Dunn McNally, February 16, 2012.

162 Veilleux, interview.

163 See http://www.cristoreynetwork.org/.

164 Thomas P. O'Neill III, "Cristo Rey's timeless lesson," *The Boston Herald*, December 17, 2011.

165 Cara Stillings Candal and Charles L. Glenn, "Race Relations in an Evangelical and a Catholic Urban High School," *Journal of School Choice: International Research and Reform*, 6, no. 1 (2011).

166 See http://www.cristoreynetwork.org/.

167 Jeff Thielman, interview with the author, January 18, 2012.

168 Interview with William McKersie, January 24, 2012.

169 Thielman, interview.

170 See ndhslaw.org.

171 See cristoreyboston.org and ndcrhs.org.

172 Candal and Glenn, "Race Relations."

173 Data provided by Boston Cristo Rey.

174 See cristoreyboston.org, ndcrhs.org, and Boston Public Schools at a Glance, 2010-11.

175 See https://www.bls.gov/news.release/hsgec.nr0.htm.

176 McKersie, interview.

177 Data provided by Cristo Rey Boston.

178 Ibid.

179 Stephen Hughes, interview with the author, January 13, 2012.

180 Ibid.

181 Ibid.

182 Mary Jo Keaney, interview with the author, January 18, 2012.

183 See https://www.federationforchildren.org/guidebook/ and https://www.edchoice.org/research/win-win-solution/.

184 National Center for Education Statistics. 2017. "Mapping State Proficiency Standards." https://nces.ed.gov/nationsreportcard/ studies/statemapping/.

185 National Center for Education Statistics. 2018. "Program for International Student Assessment (PISA)." https://nces.ed.gov/ surveys/pisa/; "Trends in International Mathematics and Science Study (TIMSS)." https://nces.ed.gov/timss/.

186 U.S. Census Bureau. "2011 American Community Survey 5-Year Estimates."

187 See "#1 for Some," at https://number1forsome.org/wp-content/ uploads/sites/16/2018/09/Number-1-for-Some-9.25-18.pdf.

188 Massachusetts Constitution, Article XVIII, Section 2.

189 Ira Lupu, "The Blaine Game: Controversy Over the Blaine Amendments and Public Funding of Religion." Pew Research: Religion & Public Life Project. July 24, 2008. See also: Institute for Justice, "Arizona Parents Defend School Choice From Education Establishment's Third Legal Attack," see http://www. ij.org/arizona-corporate-tax-credit-scholarships-background.

190 See *Arizona Christian School Tuition Organization v. Winn*, 131 S. Ct. 1436 (2011).

191 See *Kotterman v. Killian*, 972 P.2d 606 (Arizona, 1999).

192 See EdChoice, "The ABCs of School Choice," January 22, 2020, https://www.edchoice.org/research/the-abcs-of-school-choice/.

193 EdChoice, "Utah — Special Needs Opportunity Scholarship Program," https://www.edchoice.org/school-choice/programs/ utah-special-needs-opportunity-scholarship-program/.

194 EdChoice, "The 123s of School Choice," at https://www.edchoice. org/research/the-123s-of-school-choice/.

195 Ibid.

196 Andrew J. Coulson, "Comparing Public, Private, and Market Schools: The International Evidence," *The Journal of School Choice*, Volume 3, Issue 1, 2009.

197 See https://nces.ed.gov/programs/schoolchoice/ind_08.asp.

198 See https://www.edchoice.org/wp-content/uploads/2018/10/2018-10-Surveying-Florida-Scholarship-Families-byJason-Bedrick-and-Lindsey-Burke.pdf.

199 See https://www.cato.org/publications/commentary/low-income-parents-highly-satisfied-new-hampshires-scholarship-tax-credits.

200 See EdChoice, "The 123s of School Choice."

201 David Figlio and Cassandra Hart, "Does Competition Improve Public Schools?" Education Next, Winter, 2011. See http://educationnext.org/does-competition-improve-public-schools/.

202 Ibid.

203 EdChoice, *The ABC's of School Choice: The Comprehensive Guide to Every Private School Choice Program in America*, 2020 ed. (Indianapolis: EdChoice, 2020), https://www. edchoice.org/abcs.

204 Martin F. Lueken (2020). The Fiscal Impact of K-12 Educational Choice: Using Random Assignment Studies of Private School Choice Programs to Infer Student Switcher Rates, *Journal of School Choice*, posted online March 2020, retrieved from: https://doi.org/10.1080/15582159.2020.1735863.

205 Martin F. Lueken (2018). The fiscal effects of tax-credit scholarship programs in the United States, *Journal of School Choice*, 12 (2), 181-215, retrieved from https://doi.org/10.1080/15 582159.2018.1447725.

206 Charles M. North, "Estimating the Savings to Arizona Taxpayers of the Private School Tuition Tax Credit," Baylor University, November 2009.

207 Andrew LeFevre, "A Decade of Success: Pennsylvania's Education Improvement Tax Credit," Commonwealth Foundation. *Policy Brief*, Vol. 23, No. 8, August 2011.

208 Martin F. Lueken (2019). *Projected Fiscal Impact of Pennsylvania Senate Bill No. 299*, EdChoice Brief, May 14, 2019, retrieved from: https://www.edchoice.org/wp-content/uploads/2019/06/EdChoice-brief_PA-SB-299-fiscal-projections.pdf.

209 Office of Program Policy Analysis and Government Accountability. "Florida Tax Credit Scholarship Program: Fiscal Year 2008-09 Fiscal Impact," March 1, 2010.

210 EdChoice. *The ABC's of School Choice: The Comprehensive Guide to Every Private School Choice Program in America*, 2020 ed. (Indianapolis: EdChoice, 2020), https://www.edchoice.org/wp-content/uploads/2020/01/2020-ABCs-of-School-Choice-WEB-OPTIMIZED-REVISED.pdf.

211 Authors' estimates based on data from EdChoice: "School Choice in America Dashboard," EdChoice, last modified February 4, 2020 http://www.edchoice.org/school-choice/school-choice-in-america.

212 Note that school districts that spend more than the required amount may choose to reduce expenditures.

213 U.S. Census Bureau, *2018 Annual Survey of School System Finances*, https://www.census.gov/data/tables/2018/econ/school-finances/secondary-education-finance.html.

214 U.S. Department of Education, National Center for Education Statistics, Common Core of Data (CCD), "National Public Education Financial Survey (State Fiscal)," 2016-17 v.1a; "State Nonfiscal Public Elementary/Secondary Education Survey," 2018-19 v.1a.

215 About 54 percent of state and local funding for Massachusetts school districts is allocated on a student basis. Edunomics Lab, "Student Based Allocation," Georgetown University, https://edunomicslab.org/our-research/student-based-allocations/ (accessed 10/28/2020).

216 In FY 2019, required NSS exceeded the foundation budget for 269 school districts. Massachusetts Department of Elementary and Secondary Education. "Compliance with Net School Spending Requirements." See http://www.doe.mass.edu/finance/chapter70/compliance.html.

217 Local governments may also contribute above the required formula amount. Spending statewide exceeded required formula amount by 26 percent. Local decisions to raise additional revenue for K-12 generally are not based directly on enrollment, so a TCS program will likely have little or no impact in this area.

Victoria Lee and Kristin Blagg (2018), *School District Funding in Massachusetts: Computing the Effects of Changes to the Chapter 70*

Funding Formula, retrieved from Urban Institute: https://www. urban.org/sites/default/files/publication/99544/2018_12_21_ ma_school_district_funding_finalizedv2_2.pdf.

218 Massachusetts Department of Elementary and Secondary Education, "School Finance: Chapter 70 Program, FY19 Chapter 70 Aid and Required Contribution Calculations, September 2018," retrieved from: https://www.doe.mass.edu/finance/ chapter70/fy2019/whitepaper.html.

219 In FY 2019, actual NSS exceeded the district's required NSS amount for 311 of the state's 320 school districts.

Massachusetts Department of Elementary and Secondary Education, Office of School Finance, "Compliance With Net School Spending Requirements, Net School Spending (NSS) and Foundation Budget FY19 and FY20," retrieved from: https:// www.doe.mass.edu/finance/chapter70/compliance.html.

220 Notably, a TCS program would have minimal or no impact on federal funding, which is largely based on census data instead of student enrollment.

221 Roughly one-third of Massachusetts school districts receive foundation aid. Cara Stillings Candal and Ken Ardon (2019). *Charter Public School Funding in Massachusetts: A Primer*, Pioneer Institute, Policy Brief, February, retrieved from: https:// files.eric.ed.gov/fulltext/ED593774.pdf.

222 FY 2020 estimate based on MADESE data, "Chapter 70 Trends in Aid and Local Contribution," https://www.doe.mass.edu/ finance/chapter70/.

223 Between FY 2014 and FY 2020, Chapter 70 state aid increased from $4.3 million to $5.2 million while student enrollment declined over the same period. MADESE, Chapter 70 Program, "Chapter 70 Trends in Aid and Local Contribution," retrieved from: http://www.doe.mass.edu/finance/chapter70/keyfactors. xlsx.

224 Victoria Lee and Kristin Blagg (2018), *School District Funding in Massachusetts: Computing the Effects of Changes to the Chapter 70 Funding Formula*, retrieved from Urban Institute: https://www. urban.org/sites/default/files/publication/99544/2018_12_21_ ma_school_district_funding_finalizedv2_2.pdf.

225 Benjamin Scafidi, "The Fiscal Effects of School Choice Programs on Public School Districts," Friedman Foundation for Educational Choice, March 2012, 13.

226 For a brief discussion on educational costs, see Martin F. Lueken (2017), "On Educational Costs: Fixed, Quasi-fixed and Variable Costs," EdChoice, retrieved from https://www.edchoice.org/wp-content/uploads/2017/06/2017-3-Fixed-vs-Variable-Cost-One-Pager.pdf.

227 Using data from the National Center for Education Statistics, we consider the following three categorical expenditures as variable in the short run: Instruction, Instruction Support Services, and Student Support Services. We exclude other short-run variable and quasi-variable costs such as food service and transportation.

   U.S. Department of Education, National Center for Education Statistics, Common Core of Data (CCD), "National Public Education Financial Survey (State Fiscal)," 2016-17 v.1a; "School District Finance Survey (F-33)," 2016-17 (FY 2017) v.1a; "State Nonfiscal Public Elementary/Secondary Education Survey," 2018-19 v.1a.

228 See https://www.payingforseniorcare.com/federal-poverty-level.

229 Jason Bedrick, "Choosing to Learn: Scholarship Tax Credit Programs in the United States and Their Implications for New Hampshire," Josiah Bartlett Center, March 2012. See http://www.jbartlett.org/schoolchoiceweek.

230 See: http://www.privateschoolreview.com/tuition-stats/private-school-cost-by-state.

231 Florida Department of Education. "FTC Scholarship Program," September 2013.

232 Martin F. Lueken (2020). The Fiscal Impact of K-12 Educational Choice: Using Random Assignment Studies of Private School Choice Programs to Infer Student Switcher Rates, *Journal of School Choice*, posted online March 2020, retrieved from: https://doi.org/10.1080/15582159.2020.1735863.

233 This amount reflects the statewide average per-pupil amount. Because TCS participants are more likely to be low-income and ELL, this amount will likely be greater. The estimates reported under the present analysis would hold qualitatively.

234 Telephone interview with Heather Gossart, August 14, 2017.

235 Cristo Rey Network website, At a Glance, see https://www.cristoreynetwork.org/about/at-a-glance.

236 Kyle Spencer, "Catholic Schools in U.S. Court China's Youth, and Their Cash," *The New York Times*, April 6, 2014.

237 Ibid.

238 School Profiles, Cristo Rey Network website, viewed August 21, 2017.

239 Jonathan Petersen, Putting Education to Work: An Interview with Fr. John Foley, Founder of Cristo Rey, Bible Gateway Blog, August 22, 2014, see https://www.biblegateway.com/blog/2014/08/putting-education-to-work-an-interview-with-fr-john-foley-founder-of-cristo-rey/.

240 Ibid.

241 CBS "60 Minutes" feature on Cristo Rey Jesuit, 2004. https://www.cristoreynetwork.org/resources/videos.

242 See Cristo Rey Network website, At a Glance.

243 FAQs, at https://www.cristoreynetwork.org/about/faqs.

244 Telephone interview with Meagan Chuckran, Director of Performance Measurement, Cristo Rey Network, August 23, 2017.

245 U.S. Department of Labor, Part 570—Child Labor Regulations, Orders and Statements of Interpretation, see www.ecfr.gov.

246 Telephone interview with Elizabeth Goettl, August 23, 2017.

247 "Cristo Rey Schools Bring Promise of Catholic Education to Those Who Can't Afford It," National Catholic Register, September 12, 2016.

248 Telephone interview with Fr. John Foley, July 19, 2017.

249 Telephone interview with B.J. Cassin, July 17, 2017.

250 Ibid.

251 Cristo Rey High School Boston 2016 Annual Report, 7.

252 Telephone interview with John O'Keeffe, August 4, 2017.

253 Cristo Rey High School Boston 2016 Annual Report, 11.

254 Cristo Rey High School Boston 2015 Annual Report, 4.

255 Notre Dame Cristo Rey High School 2015–2016 Annual Report, 23.

256 Chuckran, telephone interview.

257 Telephone interview with Sr. Maryalyce Gilfeather, July 24, 2017.

258 Telephone interview with Heather Gossart, August 14, 2017.

259 Telephone interview with Carrie Wagner, July 31, 2017.

260 Seanna Mullen Sumrak, via email, August 7, 2017.

261 Telephone interview with Sr. Maryalyce Gilfeather, July 24, 2017.

262 Telephone interview with Carrie Wagner, July 31, 2017.

263 Ibid.

264 Ibid.

265 Telephone interview with Elena Zongrone, August 4, 2017.

266 Telephone interview with Rebecca Twitchell, August 9, 2017.

267 Megan Sweas, *Putting Education to Work: How Cristo Rey High Schools Are Transforming Urban Education*, (New York: HarperOne, 2014, 29).

268 Executive Summary, "Report on the Feasibility of a Cristo Rey Model High School in the Archdiocese of Boston, MA," 13.

269 While public school options such as charter schools now exist in most states, they are by no means widely available in all places. Further, while parents are guaranteed the right to choose among schools, many are prevented from using government money for a private school education. See "How Does School Choice Work in Other Countries?" The Friedman Foundation for Educational Choice.

270 Bruce D. Baker, Danielle Farrie, and David Sciarra, "Is School Funding Fair? A National Report Card," third edition (Newark, New Jersey: Education Law Center, 2014).

271 Frances C. Fowler, "Introduction: The Great School Choice Debate," The Clearing House: A Journal of Educational Strategies, Issues and Ideas, 76 (1) (2002), 4-7.

272 States also offer personal tax credits that could theoretically allow private school choice. The tax credits serve the largest number of families (almost 300,000 in Illinois alone), but they are almost always small relative to private school tuition and therefore do not actually materially affect school choice.

273 See "School Choice Guidebook, 2019," American Federation for Children, Washington D.C., https://www.federationforchildren.org/wp-content/uploads/2019/09/AFC-2019-School-Choice-Guidebook.pdf.

274 METCO, 2018-19 Annual Report, https://metcoinc.org/home/annual-report/.

275 Private School Universe Survey, National Center for Education Statistics, U.S. Department of Education, accessible at https://nces.ed.gov/surveys/pss/tables1112.asp.

276 American Community Survey data reported by Kids Count Data Center. See http://datacenter.kidscount.org/data/ tables/65-median-family-income-among-households-with-children#detailed/2/2-52/false/36/any/365.

277 Distribution of Total Population by Federal Poverty Level, Kaiser Family Foundation. See http://kff.org/other/state-indicator/distribution-by-fpl/#.

278 Erin Tiernan and Alexi Cohan, "Private schools seeing bump in enrollment interest as coronavirus pushes public schools to go remote," *Boston Herald*, August 10, 2020.

279 See http://pioneerinstitute.org/school_choice/poll-finds-likely-massachusetts-voters-overwhelmingly-favor-more-school-choice/.

280 See https://www.federationforchildren.org/national-school-choice-poll-shows-67-of-voters-support-school-choice-2019/.

281 Ball et al. "Manufacturing Success: Improved Access to Vocational Education in Massachusetts," Northeastern University School of Law, March 26, 2014. See also: Megan Woolhouse, "Schools' wait lists called a drag on the economy," *The Boston Globe*, September 25, 2014.

282 Ibid.

283 Massachusetts Department of Elementary and Secondary Education (DESE), Office of School Finance, "School choice trends in enrollment and tuition," http://www.doe.mass.edu/finance/schoolchoice/.

284 Michael Coulter, "Public School Choice Grows in Massachusetts," *Heartlander*, October 1, 2005. See http://news.heartland.org.

285 See http://www.doe.mass.edu/metco/.

286 Susan Eaton and Gina Chirichigno, "METCO Merits More: The History and Status of METCO," (Boston: Pioneer Institute, 2011); See also Laura J. Nelson, "METCO Students on Positive

Track: Study Says They Outperform Their Peers." *Boston Globe*, June 16, 2011.

287 Kate Apfelbaum and Kenneth Ardon, "Expanding METCO and Closing Achievement Gaps," (Boston: Pioneer Institute, white paper No. 129, March 2015).

288 Massachusetts DESE "METCO Frequently Asked Questions," see http://www.doe.mass.edu/metco/faq.html?section=all.

289 Apfelbaum and Ardon.

290 Gerard Robinson and Edwin Chang, "The Color of Success: Black Student Achievement in Public Charter Schools," Issue Brief for the National Alliance for Public Charter Schools, 2008.

291 See "Charter School Performance in Massachusetts," Center for Research on Educational Outcomes (CREDO) (Stanford University, February 28, 2013).

292 Massachusetts DESE "Charter school fact sheet, directory and application history," 2019-2020," http://www.doe.mass.edu/charter/factsheet.html.

293 Ibid.

294 Cara Stillings Candal, "Innovation Interrupted: How the Achievement Gap Act of 2010 Has Redefined Charter Public Schooling in Massachusetts," (Boston: Pioneer Institute, white paper No. 126, December 2014).

295 Stephen Q. Cornman, Thomas Stewart, and Patrick J. Wolf, "The Evolution of School Choice Consumers: Parent and Student Voices on the Second Year of the D.C. Opportunity Scholarship Program," Georgetown University School Choice Demonstration Project, May 2007; See also Paul DiPerna, "Schooling in America Survey: What Do Mothers Say About K–12 Education?" Friedman Foundation for Educational Choice, May 8, 2013.

296 Patrick J. Wolf, "School Voucher Programs: What the Research Says About Parental School Choice," *BYU Law Review*, 2008 (2).

297 Research could also be biased if one set of schools had higher dropout or expulsion rates — e.g. if private schools expelled all low performing students then the test results would be artificially inflated. The most carefully conducted studies allow for this possibility and still find positive effects from vouchers.

298 Patrick J. Wolf, "Civics Exam: Schools of Choice Boost Civics Values." *Education Next*, 7 (3), May 2007; See also Jay P. Greene, Jonathan N. Mills, and Stuart Buck, "The Milwaukee Parental Choice Program's Effect on School Integration, SCDP Milwaukee Evaluation Report #20." Fayetteville, Arkansas: School Choice Demonstration Project, 2010.

299 Caroline Hoxby, "School Choice and School Productivity (or Could School Choice Be a Tide that Lifts All Boats?)" National Bureau for Economic Research Working Paper No. 8873. See also: [1] Clive R. Belfield and Henry M. Levin, "The Effects of Competition on Educational Outcomes: A Review of U.S. Evidence," National Center for the Study of the Privatization of Education, Teachers College, Columbia University, New York, New York, 2002; [2] Timothy R. Sass, "Charter Schools and Student Achievement in Florida," *Education Finance and Policy*, 1 (1), 2006; [3] Terry M. Moe, "Beyond the Free Market: The Structure of School Choice," *Brigham Young University Law Review*, 2008:2.

300 Nathan L. Gray, John D. Merrifield, and Kerry A. Adzima, "A private universal voucher program's effects on traditional public schools," *Journal of Economics and Finance*, published online, 2014.

301 See, for example, "TIMSS Results Place Massachusetts Among World Leaders in Math and Science," Massachusetts DESE, December 9, 2008. See http://www.doe.mass.edu/news/news.aspx?id=4457.

302 Candal, 2014.

303 Ball et al., 2014.

304 Rita Anne O'Neill, "The School Voucher Debate After Zelman: Can States Be Compelled to Fund Sectarian Schools Under the Federal Constitution?" *Boston College Law Review* (4, 4/5), 2003.

305 Kenneth Ardon and Jason Bedrick, "Giving Kids Credit: Using Scholarship Tax Credits to Increase Educational Opportunity in Massachusetts," (Boston: Pioneer Institute, white paper No. 119, July 2014).

306 Data from the Current Population Survey indicate that 70 percent of families sending children to private schools in Massachusetts have income greater than twice the poverty line.

307 This figure assumes that one-third of the vouchers went to high school students and two-thirds went to K-8 students.

308 Robert Costrell, "Who Gains, Who Loses? The Fiscal Impact of the Milwaukee Parental Choice Program," *Education Next*, Winter 2009, Volume 9, No 1.

309 For a discussion of the disparate impact of a change in enrollment on funding, see Ardon and Bedrick (2014). Reducing state aid based on Chapter 70 would also mean that the net cost of vouchers would depend on which districts lost students.

310 Cara Stillings Candal and Ken Ardon, "Attrition, Dropout, and Student Mobility in District and Charter Schools: A Demographic Report," (Boston: Pioneer Institute, white paper No. 164, January 2017).

311 "Catholic Schools: Communities of Academic Excellence," NCEA Parent News, National Catholic Education Association, July 2016.

312 Heather Gossart, telephone interview, April 7, 2017.

313 Kathy Mears, telephone interview, May 2, 2017.

314 Office of Career/Vocational Technical Education, Massachusetts Department of Elementary & Secondary Education (DESE).

315 David Ferreira, telephone interview, February 10, 2017.

316 Press release, Office of Governor Charlie Baker, January 22, 2016.

317 "Governor Baker announces $9.3 Million towards VocTech training, equipment," Feb. 29, 2016, The Official Blog of the Office of the Governor of Massachusetts.

318 Press release, "Baker-Polito Administration Awards $11.8 Million in Workforce Skills Capital Grants," Office of Governor Charlie Baker, March 3, 2017.

319 Catherine Tumber, Barry Bluestone, et al., "The Critical Importance of Vocational and Technical Education in the Commonwealth," Northeastern University School of Public Policy & Urban Affairs, January 2016.

320 Ibid, 6.

321 DESE, "Massachusetts Chapter 74 Career/Vocational Technical Education Program Directory," 6-12, January 2016.

322 Massachusetts Executive Office of Labor and Workforce Development.

323 Ernest Houle, telephone interview, March 8, 2017.

324 John Lafleche, telephone interview, March 21, 2017.

325 Edward A. Bouquillon, telephone interview, March 7, 2017.

326 Ferreira, telephone interview.

327 James Vaznis, "As applications drop, BC High School ponders its future," *Boston Globe*, May 6, 2017.

328 "The State of Catholic Schools in the US," *The Catholic World Report*, May 31, 2011.

329 Ibid.

330 Mears, telephone interview.

331 Boston College; Endicott College; UMass, Dartmouth; Northeastern University; University of Massachusetts, Amherst, etc.

332 Victoria Kelly, telephone interview, April 10, 2017.

333 "Graduate Statistics," Mercy Career & Technical High School website.

334 "Forging Futures with Faith and Focus," Mercy Career & Technical High School 2016 Annual Report.

335 Ibid.

336 Nurse Aide Training Program, Mercy website.

337 Letter written by the mother of a private school student, February 2018.

338 United States Department of Education (USED) Office of Special Education and Rehabilitative Services, History: Twenty-Five Years of Progress in Educating Children With Disabilities Through IDEA, modified July 19, 2007, accessed February 23, 2018.

339 USED, Provisions Related to Children With Disabilities Enrolled by Their Parents in Private Schools (March 2011), 1.

340 USED, "The IDEA 40th Anniversary: 40 Years of the Individuals with Disabilities Education Act (IDEA)." See https://www2.ed.gov/about/offices/list/osers/idea40/index.html.

341 In education law, LEAs are equivalent to school districts. For example, the Boston Public School District is the Boston LEA.

342 Massachusetts Department of Elementary and Secondary Education (DESE), Grants and Other Financial Assistance Programs: FY2018: Individuals with Disabilities Education Act (IDEA) Federal Special Education Entitlement Grant, updated August 16, 2017. See http://www.doe.mass.edu/grants/2018/240/.

343 USED, Questions and Answers on Serving Children With Disabilities Placed by Their Parents at Private Schools, revised April 2011.

344 The formula for determining proportionate share is based on the total number of eligible private school children with special needs aged 3 through 21 attending private schools located in the LEA in relation to the total number of eligible public and private school children with disabilities aged 3 through 21 within the LEA.

345 This amendment occurred to the Massachusetts Constitution in 1855. Along with New York, Massachusetts was the first state to adopt such an amendment. Cf. U.S. Commission on Civil Rights, The Blaine Amendments & Anti-Catholicism, 2007, 5, 35, 43, 53.

346 Commonwealth of Massachusetts, Constitution, Article XVIII, Section 2.

347 DESE, MA 603 CMR 28:03, e, 4.

348 DESE, 2017-18 Selected Populations Report, accessed February 23, 2018.

349 Carole Thomson, unpublished letter to PACE & BJE, November 16, 2007.

350 Ruth E. Ryder, letter to Ellen Chambers, December 27, 2016.

351 DESE, MA 603 CMR 28:03 (1) (e), accessed February 23, 2018.

352 Stephen Perla, interview, November 8, 2017.

353 Elizabeth O'Connell, interview, December 12, 2017.

354 Lisa Moy, interview, November 28, 2017.

355 Not all students had IEPS, however. Some had undergone private testing while others, suspected of having a disability, had been informally identified by the private school staff.

356 Ariella Hellman, Nancy Kriegel, David Perda, Sr. Andrea Ciszewski, Stephen Perla, PRS Complaint, June 27, 2017, Appendix J., unpublished.

357 Ibid., Section III, 7-8.

358 Ibid., Section III.

359 Barry Barnett (Director, PRS), memorandum to Jeff Wulfson (Acting Commissioner, DESE), November 20, 2017, unpublished.

360 Hellman et. alia, Section IV, pg. 7.

361 *Zobrest v. Catalina Foothills School District*, 509 U.S.1 (February 24, 1993 – June 18, 1993), see https://www.law.cornell.edu/supct/html/92-94.ZS.html.

362 *Bloom vs. School Committee of Springfield*, 376 Mass. 35 (February 15, 1978 – July 20, 1978, Hampden County, MA), http://masscases.com/cases/sjc/376/376mass35.html February 23, 2018.

363 *Attorney General vs. School Committee of Essex*, 387 Mass. 26 (May 3, 1982 – August 31, 1982, Essex County, MA) http://masscases.com/cases/sjc/387/387mass326.html# February 23, 2018.

364 This three-part test looks at whether (1) the purpose of the grant is to aid the private institution, (2) the grant "substantially" aids the private institution and (3) the grant "avoids the risks of the political and economic abuses that prompted the passage of the Anti-Aid Amendment." *George Caplan v. Town of Acton*, SJC-12274, slip. op. at 3 (September 7, 2017 – March 9, 2018).

365 In the latest reauthorization of ESSA, a state ombudsman has been appointed to ensure that private school students receive equitable services.

366 U.S. Census Bureau, The Opportunity Atlas, https://www.opportunityatlas.org/.

367 George Weigel, "The Educational Pilgrimage of JPII and its Impact on the World."

368 Ibid.

369 Sean McCarroll, "The Plenary Councils of Baltimore (1852-1884): The Formation of America's Catholic School System Amidst Anti-Catholicism in the United States," paper written for History 397.001, Fall 2011; Charles Leslie Glenn, Jr., *The Myth of the Common School* (Amherst, Massachusetts: University of Massachusetts Press, 1988).

370 Tim Keller, "Myth: Private School Choice is Unconstitutional," *School Choice Myths: Setting the Record Straight on Education Freedom*, edited by Corey A. DeAngelis and Neal P. McCluskey (Cato Institute, Washington, D.C., 2020).

371 *Pierce v. Society of Sisters*, 268 U.S. 510 (more) 45 S. Ct. 571; 69 L. Ed. 1070; 1925.

372 Richard J. Murnane, Sean F. Reardon, Preeya P. Mbekeani, and Anne Lamb, "Who Goes to Private School? Long-term Enrollment Trends by Family Income," *Education Next*, 18 (4), 2018, 61.

373 David E. Campbell, *Civic Education: Readying Massachusetts' Next Generation of Citizens*, Pioneer Institute for Public Policy, white paper No. 17, 2001; Patrick J. Wolf, "Civics Exam: Schools of Choice Boost Civic Values," *Education Next* 7 (3), 2007, pp. 66-72; Christian Smith and David Sikkink, "Is Private Schooling Privatizing?" *First Things 92* (April), 1999, pp. 16-20; Patrick Wolf and Stephen Macedo, with David Ferrero and Charles Venegoni (editors), *Educating Citizens: International Perspectives on Civic Values and School Choice* (Washington, D.C: Brookings Institution, 2004).

374 Julie Trivitt and Patrick J. Wolf, "School Choice and the Branding of Catholic Schools," *Education Finance and Policy*, 6 (2), 2011, 202-245.

375 Corey A. DeAngelis, Patrick J. Wolf, Larry D. Maloney, and Jay F. May, *Charter School Funding: Inequity Surges in the Cities*, School Choice Demonstration Project, University of Arkansas, Fayetteville, 2020.

376 Murnane et al., 59.

377 Marisa Schultz, "Education Secretary DeVos Warns about Wave of Private School Closings: 'That's a Crisis in the Making,'" Fox News, September 19, 2020.

378 COVID-19 Permanent Private School Closures, Cato Institute, accessed on October 25, 2020.

379 Kristina Rex, "With In-Person Learning, Massachusetts Catholic Schools See Surge in Enrollment," WBZ4 CBS Boston, September 16, 2020.

380 Albert Cheng, Patrick J. Wolf, Wendy Wang, and W. Bradford Wilcox, *The Protestant Family Ethic: What do Protestant, Catholic, Private, and Public Schooling Have to do with Marriage, Divorce, and Non-marital Childbearing?* Institute for Family Studies, American Enterprise Institute, Washington, D.C.

381 591 U. S. _____ (2020), p. 20.

382 *Zelman v. Simmons-Harris*, 536 U.S. 639 (2002).

383 David Sharp, "Maine Ban on Tuition Payments to Religious Schools is Upheld," AP News, October 30, 2020.

384 Meghan Mangrum, "Tennessee Court of Appeals Upholds Decision Finding Gov. Bill Lee's Education Savings Account Program Unconstitutional," *Nashville Tennessean*, September 29, 2020.

385 Matthew M. Chingos, Daniel Kuehn, Tomas Monarrez, Patrick J. Wolf, John F. Witte, and Brian Kisida, *The Effects of Means-tested Private School Choice Programs on College Enrollment and Graduation*. Urban Institute Research Report, Washington, D.C., 2019.

386 Corey A. DeAngelis and Lindsey Burke, "Does Regulation Induce Homogenisation? An Analysis of Three Voucher Programmes in the United States," *Journal of School Choice*, 23 (7-8), 2017, 311-327.

387 Tweet of Pope Francis, March 1, 2014.